Praise for Another

MW00464937

"Whoever says miracles don't happen hasn't met the Lewis brothers! This story is a perfect example of how a loving God is orchestrating his will in the lives of the men and women he created. Our physical bodies are not our own, but a temporary gift given to us for a higher purpose. Trust in the Lord with all your heart and he will direct your paths!
I am honored to have shared this story with Mid-Michigan."
>   *-Jessica Harthorn,*
>   Television News Reporter

"I'm so glad you are writing a book about this! This is one of the most God-involved true stories I have ever heard. May God bless this work!!"
>   -Barb Julian (Donors Mom)
>   Phoenix, AZ

"It was my privilege to get to hear Troy's story first hand – and watch the Lord speak through him to our congregation that Sunday morning. As Troy would say, it really is "God's story" more than "Troy's story" anyway! As a result of that Sunday morning interview, which was part of my message, we sold more sermon CD's that day than any day before or since. It truly is an amazing and inspiring story, and countless people have been moved and touched by it."
>   *-Pastor Scott Park*
>   *Impact Christian Church*
>   *Woodland Park, CO*

"Troy's journey of illness, struggle and disappointment was the circumstance God used to reveal His power to work all things together for Troy's good and God's glory. His story inspires all of us not to give up."
-Pastor Bob Hinz
Bedford Alliance Church
Temperance, Michigan

"Troy Lewis has hit a grand slam with *"Another Second Chance: God's Story."* His honest telling of our miracle working God that touched him, his devoted wife, and his whole family will be a delight to all! Troy's enthusiasm for serving and honoring the Lord is infectious and will grab your heart right from page one! In a simple and understandable manner, Troy humbly encourages everyone reading this book that no matter what we face in life; we can all experience a revelation of a Loving Father that is working out His Story in each one of our lives. It is both a pleasure and a privilege to recommend this book, I pray it brings immeasurable hope and imparts supernatural strength to the reader to endure and stand fast in the Lord in whatever season of trial they may be going through."
-Lori Young
Anchored to the Rock
Christian Family Store
Fremont, OH

ANOTHER SECOND CHANCE

...God's Story

To Laura,
May the God
of Second Chances
Bless You Always!

Troy Lewis

BY
TROY LEWIS

Rom 8:28

~ 3 ~

Coe 2:9

© 2011 by Troy Lewis. All rights reserved.

Writing Career Coach Press (a division of Writing Career Coach, 14665 Fike Rd., Riga, MI 49276) functions only as book publisher. As such, the ultimate design, content, editorial accuracy, and views expressed or implied in this work are those of the author.

No part of this publication may be reproduced, stored in a retrieval system, or transmitted in any way by any means—electronic, mechanical, photocopy, recording, or otherwise—without the prior permission of the copyright holder, except as provided by USA copyright law.

ISBN 13: 978-0-9833607-7-3

ISBN 10: 0983360774

Scriptures taken from the Holy Bible, New International Version®, NIV®. Copyright © 1973, 1978, 1984, 2011 by Biblica, Inc.™ Used by permission of Zondervan. All rights reserved worldwide. www.zondervan.com.

The "NIV" and "New International Version" are trademarks registered in the United States Patent and Trademark Office by Biblica, Inc.™

I prayerfully dedicate this book

To the One that inspired me to share these words

He has many names

Hope, Love, Elohim, I am, Yahweh, Jesus, Jehovah,

The Holy Sovereign Creator of the universe

God

Table of Contents

"I consider that our present sufferings are not worth comparing

with the glory that will be revealed in us."

- *Romans 8:18*

1

God's Story

"It's probably nothing serious, but you might want to get it checked out."

These are the words that I heard from a nurse standing in my house in 1992. These words would act as the "seed" to this incredible story.

I didn't know it then, but these words would lead to a defining moment in my life. A trial that I would be forced to go through. That would cause me to question who I was, all that I had believed, and God himself.

I had played Jesus Christ in a passion drama for nine years, the same drama that brought me to the Lord in 2001. I was also a successful girl's fast pitch softball coach for seven years, coaching girls from 10 & under all the way to the high school level.

I am a service manager for a fire sprinkler contractor in Toledo, OH and have worked there for 20 years. I am married to a lovely lady and have two beautiful daughters.

But in 2010, I was left standing on the outside looking in, as I came to the realization...

"Life as I knew it was over".

I would begin a race against time to go on dialysis and get a kidney transplant as my kidneys began to shut down. Only to find out, that the one thing that was supposed to keep me alive, was actually killing me.

The journey would be filled with many twists, turns, detours, and road blocks. There were many times that I would ask God "why me" and "where are you going with this?"

It wasn't until he delivered me through the valley of the shadow of death, through incredible odds and miraculous events. It was then that I realized "why this happened to me".

It was to write this book, and to share with you the hope of what I know to be true. In my darkest moment, as I lay on death's door step. Hope showed up in a miraculous way! That is the same hope that is with you through all of your trials.

This story is not just about me. This story is your own as well. My battle was life and death as my kidneys began to shut down. Yours may have been another health issue, the loss of a loved one, the changing of a career, or some other trial that was unforeseen.

This book is going to be a little bit different than some you may have read. This story is one that I lived.

I hope as you read through the pages you will insert you own moments of fear, possible loss, pain, heart break, surrender, and ultimately, victory.

We have all experienced these moments of suffering in life, at one time or another. I want you to know that you're not alone in yours, there is hope. Hope will allow you to persevere when things look there bleakest. It will allow you to grow and make this moment of trial into a moment of victory.

We all have a story to tell, your experience may be the inspiration that gives "Another 2nd Chance" to someone else.

God's time is not like our time nor are his ways like our ways.

Sometimes I look back over the things that happened and marvel at all of the incredible events that took place. Events that were taking place years earlier. Events taking place half way across the nation. These things had to fall into place to create this incredible story, all leading up to one main event in July of 2010.

Just when I counted on a brother's love to save me, it was a Father's love that saved us both. A thousand miles away, a stranger stepped up and courageously gave with nothing expected in return.

I could not have imagined what God had in store for all who were part of this story. Hollywood couldn't have scripted it and got away with it. This is a story that is written in the lives of all involved by the sovereign Creator of the universe.

This is God's Story!

Hope is defined as "the confidant expectation of good" and it is on that theme I'll start my tale.

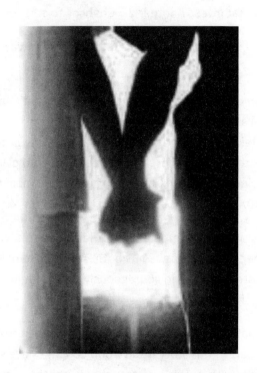

2

In the Beginning

It was 1992 and my world was going through many changes. My wife Stephanie and I bought a house, got married, and had our first daughter. I found out I had a rare kidney disease, and watched my mom go to be with the Lord just before Christmas...

On May 21, I took a young blonde-haired, brown-eyed beauty across the Indiana state line to be my everything.

It wasn't exactly the wedding a girl dreams of while she's growing up. One filled with white gowns and a ballroom of adoring family, but in our situation time was of the essence. Our little bundle of joy was set to arrive in a week, so we decided to do the inevitable and get married.

Corrine was born **seven** days later on a warm sunny spring day at **8:18** am.

When I looked down at our little Corrine, she was so precious, so lovely. I was sure she must be a gift from God. How can you be proud of a baby who has done nothing but draw their first breath? I'm not sure, but I was.

While I wasn't someone who was very involved in church at the moment, looking down at that little baby did something to me. Something so beautiful could not have been an accident. I was completely convinced that she must have been sent for a reason.

My brother Toby had always told me my mom hung on as long as she did just to see her baby (me) married and become a father. I believe I would have to agree with my brother. My mom amazed me with the amount of energy she had during those last six months of her battle with emphysema.

As a new father, it was time to start being responsible and planning for the future. I contacted a financial adviser to set us up with some life insurance in the event that the unthinkable would happen to Stephanie or me. Such an event seemed impossibly far away. I was in great physical shape, twenty-four years old and very healthy.

If you've ever bought insurance, you know how the process went. The advisor led me through a series of steps that began with filling out paperwork in his rustic office. He'd turn all the forms in and then a nurse would come out to our house to perform a brief physical to insure we were both in good physical condition. Once this part was complete, we would sign some more papers. That was all there was to it.

It seemed very seamless, so we scheduled the nurse to show up at our humble little home, to perform the tests that she needed to.

After she arrived and was settled in, she began with Stephanie. She started with all of her vitals and asking routine questions that she then wrote down on her form for the company. When she got to me, it was an almost identical process.

"You have protein in your urine," she commented.

The statement caught me off guard. She didn't seem worried by it. She was more informing me than anything else.

"Well, I've been working out, so I drink protein shakes before I lift weights," I said.

"No, that wouldn't cause this." She chuckled while writing down a few notes. "It means that there is blood in your urine. There are a few things that can cause it. It could be a kidney stone." She finished putting her stuff away.

"It's probably nothing serious, but you might want to get it checked out."

"Thanks. I will," I said, not sure how one was supposed to respond to that.

"I am going to give you guys my approval and you will be receiving your life insurance."

She then packed up all of her things and we said our goodbyes.

^^

We saw our first of two Dr. Kim's. The first was a urologist who checked me out and said I looked good.

~ 15 ~

"The tests all came back good. There were no stones found in the urinary tract and no infection found either," he began. That was welcomed news. I was happy to think that my adventure with Dr. Kim and his office was now over, as was the concern over the protein in my urine.

"But I'd like a nephrologist to rule out anything else."

"What kind of doctor is that?" I asked.

"A kidney specialist," he said. He assured me that it was only precautionary and it was for the best. So, he gave us the name of a kidney doctor, Dr. Kim.

"Is this a relative?" I laughed and asked.

"No, just an associate."

Two weeks later we were on our way to see Dr. Kim, our new nephrologist. As we sat in the waiting room, the doctor walked out to greet us.

"Mr. Lewis, how are you?" he asked. I stood to shake his extended hand.

"Doing well Dr. Kim."

He then directed us to a small exam room where we all sat down. The room had pictures of kidneys and vascular diagrams hanging on the freshly painted walls. There was an examination table with crisp white paper on it. Files were stacked neatly on his desk.

He began with a series of questions about all different subjects.

"Has anyone in your family had kidney problems?"

"No one," I said.

"Has any one in your family ever had sugar diabetes?"

"No one," I said again.

These questions continued for a few minutes. Then, when we were finished, he scheduled some testing to be done.

A couple of weeks later, after completing all of the testing, I was back in Dr. Kim's office to get the results.

I really wasn't nervous. As I've told you before, I was healthy, I worked out regularly, was young, recently married and a Daddy. This was more of a process I had to go through, just to say I did it, more than an actual search for truth. It was like an upgraded version of a checkup. You do it with the full expectation that they'll say that you are totally normal.

Do a few tests, then I was ready to get this inconvenient part of my life behind me.

"During the course of your testing we did find something," Dr. Kim said. X-rays of my kidneys hung on a lighted wall board like some kind of strange photo.

Not the news I wanted to hear. I braced myself for the worst but continued to hope for the best.

"What you have is a very rare disease in your kidneys called Iga Nephropathy."

The name sounded intimidating enough, even without knowing what it meant. In the space of two heartbeats, I simultaneously envisioned my death and decided that this was really nothing at all. It was rare, but I'd be fine.

"Of all the kidney diseases you could possibly get, this is one of the best ones," he continued, "Because 80% of the people that get this go on to live a long healthy life and never know they have anything wrong with them."

That was the news I wanted to hear. I let my breath out slowly and continued to listen. Most people have nothing happen—that was good. The rest?

"Then there is this 20%, that when they turn around age 40, these people will go into kidney failure and end up needing a transplant."

We sat there dumbfounded. It was a lot of information to take in all at once. I could be fine, but I could be on a collision course with renal failure? Surely the shock and fear was painted on our face because Dr. Kim began painting a rosy picture of the 80%, assuming that I would be in that more likely scenario.

At this point, there was no need to worry. I'd just come in every year for a checkup to see if things changed at all. In another sixteen years, I'd likely know if I was a part of the 80 or the 20.

We wandered aimlessly to our car and got in, the shock of it still clinging to us like the reverberating silence all around. I looked out the front windshield and considered everything that had happened in this last month.

What was the future going to hold for us? Was this going to be a silent bomb that would explode in in our lives? Or, would I be a part of the 80% who had no need to worry?

Would I need a kidney transplant? Would it work? Would I, like my mom, slowly fade away with a terminal disease?

I turned the key in the ignition with the thoughts still jumbling around in my mind. We drove home in silence.

All this from getting life insurance!

***

This must be some kind of oxymoron ! You find out you have a disease that could cost you your life by applying for an insurance that pays when you lose your life.

What are the odds . . .?

***

Stephanie and I began to discuss this new piece in the puzzle we call life. She had fear and concerns. Remember, she was six years younger than me and the mom of a new baby. We were talking a major illness in her early 30s, with a teenage girl in the house.

Not only that, but what if I didn't make it. Suddenly our "Happily Ever After" was overshadowed by the "Till Death Do Us Part." The idea of this stirred up fears born of her mom's eerily similar predicament.

Her step dad, Neal Moore, was in incredibly good shape. He exercised and ate right. Did all the things "they" tell you that you are supposed to do.

"Suddenly," she said, "he came down with a rare disease that caused his organs to shut down in less than a year. He retained massive amounts of fluid in the end. Then, one day, he slipped away and he was gone," she said with tears streaming down her face.

"That was just about three and a half years ago... my mom was only 36 years old," she cried.

I sat there in complete shock. No words came out of my mouth. In fact, no words were forming in my brain. I knew exactly what she was thinking.

What if I was that 20%?

If I would be the 20%, I would be in my early 40s and she would be around 36 when this thing hit us. A rare kidney disease was no longer necessary to mess up my insides, that thought alone put my stomach in knots.

"I will be fine," I said. "I'll be part of the 80%." But how could I know that?

The words seemed to assure her just a bit, so I continued. "Nothing has changed from a few months ago until now. I'm still the same guy I was. I'm healthy and nothing will probably ever happen with all of this. The doctor didn't seem worried. You know that he is just preparing us for the worst possible scenario."

After about a week, we realized there wasn't a thing that we could do about it and it seemed like 40 was a lifetime away. So, we went along with our lives as if we would end up being in the 80%.

Our family grew again, when in August of 1995 Stephanie gave birth to our second child and youngest daughter. Our little Allison was such a pretty baby and an absolute sweetheart. Not long after that, at the age of 25, Stephanie had a hysterectomy and it was decided the four of us made a complete family.

Nothing was ever out of the ordinary. I went to my annual checkups only to hear everything was fine.

^^^

3

Happy 40th Birthday

It was now 2007 and life had been rolling along at an amazing pace. Along with playing Jesus each year in a passion drama, I had also been coaching fast pitch softball for my girls for several years. That was another passion that I had and enjoyed.

We traveled to different tournaments and played other travel teams of the same caliber. All of us enjoyed the competition and the success from all of our hard work.

During the spring of that year, we were playing in a Jr. High league and doing very well. It consisted of 34 teams from northwest Ohio and southeast Michigan. When the tournament came around, the girls were hitting on all cylinders. Taking down each opponent in stride, we ended up running the table and winning it all. I was so proud of all the girls, but was extremely proud of my daughter Allison. After pitching every game, she was voted the MVP of the Championship game.

We ended up riding that high as we went through the summer months, playing in Tournaments and having a blast!

In September, shortly after my 40th birthday, I received the news from Dr. Kim that my kidney function had fallen to 27% function. Something had obviously changed...

"Wow," the doctor said, eying my latest test results, "Your kidneys have really declined."

For more than a decade, almost two decades, these annual checkups had been nothing more than, "How do you feel? Everything looks good. See you next year." That day, the doctor looked at my results and he was saying things like, "We need to watch that," and "I need to see you every month to keep an eye on this."

The world of "It won't happen to me" was shattered in an instant. Suddenly, that 20% was me. I was the one facing the worst case scenario.

Despite nerves about the situation, I went through the fall having monthly check-ups. Then around December of 2007, the doctor began talking about doing some treatments on me if things didn't start to improve.

I went into the New Year still not feeling much different and hoping it was a good sign.

I had to accept that things were not normal for me anymore. It was a tough reality, but I approached it with a positive outlook. I truly believe attitude plays a major role in our overall health. We can have a negative attitude about things or we can be positive about them. Either way our reality doesn't change, but by being positive we become that light for someone else that may be facing similar circumstances. I also believe it allows us to be healthier since we are less depressed.

Stephanie and I were sitting in Dr. Kim's office on that bitter cold January day, when the doctor looked at my chart and then to me.

"I want to put you on a high dose of Prednisone."

"Is it really necessary?"

"At this point, I think it is. I want to warn you, there are some side effects with this treatment, as with any treatment," he said. He leaned on his arm and began to tick off the side effects on his fingers. He listed off about twenty different symptoms, and while he didn't say it this way, this is what I heard:

Your face will swell up, you'll get moon face, you'll have tons of acne, you're going to gain a ton of weight, you could get a hump on your back, your hair is going to grow excessively, you will have insomnia, you're going to have major mood swings and on and on.

"So basically you're telling me I'm going to be the elephant man?" I said bluntly.

He chuckled.

"I can't do that," I continued. "The Easter passion drama is in four months. I can't get up on the cross looking like that!"

There was NO way I wanted to have that treatment. I wasn't even sure what this was going to do for me. In fact, it sounded like this "Treatment" was going to make me feel worse than I already did.

I had said my piece, so I quit talking and listened the rest of the meeting. One of the last things he said before we left was to make sure that I keep my sodium intake below 2000 mg a day. That would decrease the severity of the symptoms.

Dr. Kim wrote out the prescription and then handed it to me. It called for going to the hospital for three injections of 1,000mg of Prednisone each day, for three days, then 100mg a day afterwards.

Now you have to understand, a normal dose is 5-10mg. A high dose is 20mg. They were going to give me 1,000mg of steroids. That sounded insane!

I didn't want to face this new form of treatment. No one wants to go through all of that. Add to that the fact that I was supposed to be Jesus in the Easter Play, something I looked forward to every year.

I was also starting a new coaching position at a local high school, as well as continuing to coach my travel team.

It just couldn't be the right thing.

By February of 2008, I was about two weeks into play practices. I had been depressed for the entire week leading up to that day. I was trying to decide whether to resign from the play or not. I did not want to go on this stuff. I was petrified, scared, in complete denial.

I rationalized that my kidney function could come back. It would do it on its own. Of course, the doctor had already given me enough information for me to know that was wrong. It doesn't come back. Once the kidney function is gone, it's gone.

It's not like a cold, or even like cancer, and it goes into remission.

"When your kidney function is gone, it's gone," he told me in a moment of tough love. "You may get a couple percentage points back, but you're not going to get much."

That medicine wasn't going to make me better at all. In fact, he told me the medicine's purpose was just trying to stop it, get it under control and quit declining.

So, on February 5th 2008, I woke up and got ready to go to work. I drug myself out to a dimly lit kitchen, sat down on the dark steps that led to the basement, and I began praying in desperation. Something inside broke open and the emotions poured like a flood.

I really believe when you're going through something hard we all try to hold our chins up for a long time. We also all come to a place where we cannot do it anymore.

That day I cried and prayed in the dark. I prayed for so long the sun was starting to come up.

I didn't care about what time it was or where I had to go. I kept praying, "Why me? Why me, God? Why has this got to happen to me?" I just kept saying that over and over.

I needed clarity, what to do. I wasn't sure where to go next. I was just devastated. Things like this happened to other people, not to me.

I cried all the tears I had and then sat there for a bit longer in the silence. It was as if God had answered my prayer, but I didn't know what that answer was. Peace washed over me but I continued to wait. I glanced over and my daughter Corrine's birth certificate was lying right there.

I looked down, and there it was 8:18, and then there was a series of numbers (14 and 28) that kept repeating. 8:18 jumped off the page like a Bible verse, so I got up and I walked through the kitchen into the living room. I sat down at the desk, pulled out the Bible and just sat there looking at it.

I'm not a person who has an experience like this often. I had one other God experience, years earlier, where something similar to this happened, but it had to do with work.

In fact, even that verse held meaning to me during this trial. It was Romans 5:3-4, "rejoice in our sufferings, for we know that suffering produces perseverance, perseverance character; and character, hope."

I looked at the Bible in my hand and waited. There was no voice, no heavenly finger that came down. All I had was the memory of that first encounter, so I went to Romans. It was a book of the Bible that seems to always speak to me. The question still aching in my heart was, "Why me?"

I began in *Romans 8:14, "because those that are led by the spirit of God are sons of God"*. It was as if God was dialoging with me. I said, "Why?" He said, "Because." Then I went down to Romans 8:18, the numbers that had brought me there. It said, *"I consider that our present sufferings are not worth comparing with the glory that will be revealed in us." (Romans 8:18, NIV).*

"Why must this happen to me?" I said.

Then I read *Romans 8:28, "And we know that in all things God works for the good of those who love him, who have been called according to his purpose." (NIV)*

I was floored. I sat there after I read the third verse and a breeze literally went over the back of my neck. And it wasn't hair standing up. It was as if somebody blew on my neck.

I stood up and started smiling. It was just an amazing experience that I won't soon forget.

I got into the truck and started driving. I had this dumb smile on my face that started to turn into laughter, which then turned to tears of joy. I knew without a shadow of a doubt that something had just happened. So, that afternoon I began my treatments.

4

We lost Our Jesus

I went to get my first 1,000 milligrams of Prednisone.

Then I went back the next day, got loaded up again. I went back the following day for my last dose of 1,000 mgs. That day they handed me a bottle and said take 100mg every day for the next six months.

^   ^   ^   ^   ^   ^   ^

Steroids impact your sleep and I was getting very little on such high doses. I was averaging about 4-5 hours a night.

In my personal life, things were in a state of flux. I'd been the JV coach and that took a great deal of energy. As soon as I left work I had to hustle to the gym or ball field for the high school girls. After that, my travel team showed up for two hours.

Running at the same time was play rehearsals two or three times a week. I wasn't getting home until about 9:30pm every night and then back up at 5 am. Or, in my case, 3-4am.

And all of this was happening while my kidney function was down to about 25%.

Somehow in the midst of coaching, play practice, and work things moved forward. I had all kinds of people praying for me from church. I was in the heart of this intense treatment when Easter rolled around that year. For seven years I'd played the part of Jesus, a task that was grueling even when I was completely healthy. Now I was battling insomnia, working essentially two jobs, and doing the play.

The "Cross of Love" was the name of the play. We would generally have three or four performances a year. I would stop cutting my hair in July to start preparing. Then there was the dieting to get up on the cross in my loin cloth.

My wife and I would show up three hours ahead of each performance just to put my make-up on. Not the kind that you might be thinking. It was bruising and scars. Then, it was wet latex that she painted all over my body. When it dried, she would take scissors and begin cutting it so that it looked like large gashes in my skin.

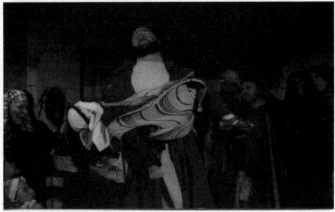

Just before the crucifixion scene, we would pour blood all over the gashes. We would also pour it on my forehead where the crown of thorns was.

Before each performance, I entered the sanctuary and walked through the scenes in my head. I then sat down in the third pew from the front, which had become my custom. It held special meaning to me. I would meditate and reflect on how this all started.

I was 33 years old when I started playing Jesus. A year prior to that, I didn't even know Him. I began to look around at the people preparing and noticed Corrine milling around. She's fifteen now and getting older. It seems like only yesterday she begged me to come here. My eyes just gazed at her until my mind drifted back to a time gone by...

*　　　*　　　*

In the spring of the year 2000, the concerns about my kidneys were only an occasional thought and then only around the time of my checkups. We lived life like everyone else.

Our little Allison was four and in preschool. Corrine was seven years old. She was in the second grade and making all kinds of friends.

There was one little guy in particular in Corrine's class who invited her to a church program called AWANAS. If you have never heard of it, it is similar to vacation Bible school but it is every Wednesday night during the school year. It is for kids, kindergarten through the 6th grade.

Stephanie and I didn't attend church. It wasn't even really something we'd ever discussed. That all changed as we continued to see the enthusiasm Corrine came home with each week. This was fun for her. Something I'd never associated with church stuff.

It wasn't long before Corrine began asking to go to church on Sundays. We really didn't like the idea of losing part of our weekend going to church. Selfish? I know that now, but at the time it was not a priority. For us Sundays were for sleeping in, going on day trips, and catching up on yard work and other things.

Corrine is a very persistent girl and kept at us. The church she was attending was having an Easter passion play and we were invited. So, we finally gave in.

This was just an evening out for us. We entered the crowded sanctuary where there were some seats available, three pews from the front. It was beautifully decorated with colorful scenery. They'd gone all out to make it feel like you were there. I was impressed.

Around us were many people chatting away, waiting in anticipation. There was electricity in the air and we were beginning to get caught up in the moment. We looked around, trying to take it all in. I had never been to anything like this. The last play I had seen was back in the 6th grade, and that's been a while, and didn't touch this. I wasn't exactly what you would call a theatrical kind of person. Heck! Who am I kidding? I couldn't even get in front of people and speak without having a panic attack.

Suddenly the lights went dim and townspeople from Jerusalem filed in from all different aisles. We were no longer in a sanctuary. We were transported back two thousand years to a village half-way around the world.

I watched Jesus perform miracles and then saw the stunned gratitude of the multitudes.

I listened to the teachings and the trial. I felt the frustration rise up in me as an innocent man, a man who only sought to HELP those around him, was unjustly accused and drug from one kangaroo court to another. The acting was powerful, moving even.

As I watched the crucifixion, something strange began to happen inside of me. Suddenly I began to see it from a different light. It was as if I was the only person in the entire church and we were in Jerusalem 2000 years ago. I began to see what Jesus Christ went through for me and all humanity. It crashed down on me. I was aware that I forced him to suffer this. Me. I forced him to be tortured and to die. It was MY sin that held him up there.

When he said "Father, forgive them for they do not know what they do" Jesus was referring to me and the way I had been living my life. This was my fault...

I became overwhelmed with emotion in my seat as I sat there with my family. Stephanie reached over and grasped my hand tenderly. She was weeping. I looked over and saw Corrine with her precious little head up against her mom's arm, hanging on to it as she sobbed. Our beautiful outfits, our lovely evening out, had instead been life changing.

There are specific moments in life, that you just know at that very instant, that things are never going to be the same again. These moments define the essence of who we are and what we will become. This was one of those moments in time for me—for our whole family really.

All day Saturday it was on my mind. I couldn't stop thinking about the crucifixion scene, how I had lived my life. Where would I go if something happened to me or even my family? But then I thought about the words that Jesus said during the play:

"I am the way and the truth and the life. No one comes to the Father except through me" (John 14:6).

I realized that if I would live more for him and less for Troy, that he would stand next to me on the day that I meet my maker. He would say "This is a child of mine, he may pass."

So, on Easter Sunday at the end of the message, the pastor began to give another invitation for anyone who wanted to accept Jesus Christ into their life to come forward.

I went forward.

"How does this work?" I asked.

"You just pray the sinner's prayer, asking Jesus to come into your heart. Asking him to forgive you of all your sins and tell him that you want to live for him from this day forward," he replied. So I prayed to accept Jesus Christ on Easter Sunday in the year 2000.

"We have lost our Jesus and we would like you to play the part."

This was the question that I was asked seven months later by Donna Miller (the Pastor's wife & play director).

"I don't sing, I don't dance, and I don't get up in front of people and speak," was my reply. Needless to say, after much prayer, I ended up doing it. I figured the Lord led me to the passion drama for a reason and this must have been it.

****

Now here I am, starting my 8th season of playing the part, all because a little eight year old girl drug me to church. I thank God she did!

This Easter (2008) ended up being the most incredible season that we had ever had. Even now I remember it. The place was standing room only. People were standing along the walls and a screen had been set up in the gymnasium for overflow. People watched the play being live streamed in from the sanctuary.

I'd done the play year after year and loved it. As I walked in each night, I tried to shake hands with every single person in the place. The song I came in to lasts about four or five minutes.

There were two rows of people with special needs, from children to adults. When I came walking in, the electricity in the room was palpable. Those two rows of people were going crazy. It was like the Super Bowl. They were cheering and screaming for Jesus. They were so sincere; it nearly brought tears to my eyes.

That night held special meaning to me because I was going to make it through. My face was a little puffy, but I'd actually lost ten pounds rather than gaining twenty-five. The stories coming out of the play were amazing.

5

Goliath Sneaks Up

In May 2008, we had to go in for my appointment to check on my progress. I almost knew the routine as well as my doctors by this point.

"Your blood pressure is 125/70." He nods. "That's really good. Usually it's a little bit higher than that."

That was good to hear. Next he checked cholesterol and it was really low. He's looking at me and he checks my ankles, weight, and blood work.

"What have you been doing?" he finally asked me.

"You told me the key was to watch my sodium. I'd been locked under 2,000 mgs every day because I didn't want to puff up."

I watched Dr. Kim type a bit more, look through my numbers, and type again. Pretty soon he was smiling and typing.

That was a good sign, right?

Dr. Kim never smiles, and now he was shaking his head, smiling and typing.

"I cannot believe it," he finally said.

"What?"

"Your function is all the way back up to 43% and it was 25%."

I said, "Yup."

This was right after the play and I was feeling like dynamite. I knew that it would work. I was going to beat this thing. I actually felt like a kid who just won the game and made his dad proud.

"That's good," he said, that smile still on his face.

"Doc, I've got to ask you." I wasn't quite sure how to ask. "I get the impression that this isn't normal. Is this a normal thing?"

"You're doing very well."

I knew things were going well. I felt good and I wasn't having all the horrible things happen we'd read about online and other places.

"Isn't that what was supposed to happen?"

I kept pressing him. He was happy about the results but I had no frame of reference. How successful had the treatment been? Finally, he said, "This isn't normal. Normally you'd get back a few notches but you don't get back 20."

"Well, I've had lots of people praying for me and I watch what I eat."

"Whatever you're doing, just keep doing it."

So I did, for awhile.

It's a good year

With the great news from Dr. Kim and the play behind us, we had the whole summer in front of us. As it turned out, I didn't swell up as bad as they'd expected. I wasn't the elephant man.

The softball team was great, too. Late in the summer, we won a tournament that qualified us for the nationals. We raised enough money through the community to take my crazy bunch of misfits down to Disney World and back.

We had a memorable time as we were introduced during opening ceremonies. The announcer started out, "To bring in our next team, can I get an 'O'". Part of the stadium went "H" "I" "O". "Coming all the way from Ohio, the Fremont Crimson Giants!"

It was AWESOME! We went and played teams from various states for several days and made a good showing.

It didn't hurt that the tournament was held at Disney World in Orlando, which is where we were all staying. It was an incredible experience that I will always cherish!

With all the celebrating, travel, and family time, I let myself relax a bit on the diet. Occasionally I'd allow myself a hotdog, a little junk food. I started pushing the threshold a little bit each time. Then pretty soon instead of only having one that day, I'd have two or three. The next thing I know, seven days a week I'm eating whatever.

2008 wore on into 2009 and life had been fairly normal. I'd been less diligent about monitoring every bite of food to cross my lips. By late 2009, I was puffing up quite a bit and it was becoming very noticeable.

∧   ∧   ∧   ∧

In the fall of 2009, we went on vacation down to a friend's lodge in southern Ohio. I was having a great time, but I noticed the longer we were down there, the more miserable I was feeling. While everyone enjoyed the warm days and crisp, cool nights, my joints stiffened up and it seemed as if every action took additional effort.

Maybe I should have thought something was wrong. But who really wants to take the good times and ruin them with what-ifs. By the final day, I couldn't stand it. I could barely move around and I was so tired I felt like I was going to pass out.

Maybe it was no more than a downswing, I reasoned. Things had been going so well. I had no reason for any concern. Lots of people get fall colds and I was sure that was all I was dealing with.

I barely made it to the car when it was time to leave. We were down by Cincinnati, which is a solid four hour drive from where we live. Stephanie drove and I pretty much slept the whole way.

"I don't feel good," I said. It seemed obvious, but sometimes you just say what you're thinking.

"We'll get home and rest and you'll feel better," Steph said.

I don't really think either one of us realized how bad it was at that point. When things are happening slowly, over the course of a year or so, it is like the frog in the pot who never tries to escape as he's slowly boiled.

We simply adjust to new versions of normal and it is only in retrospect that we realize what's happened. Think about your own life. You know you cannot do all of the same things you could do five or ten years ago. You don't worry about it. You see it as a part of the aging process. You accept it and continue. So, how much was kidneys, how much was a possible cold, and how much was age? I didn't want to believe how much of it was kidneys.

The next day, I had my regular blood work and checkup. I was still rundown from the trip, but nothing in me said to stay home from work. Still believing I was adjusting to the new normal, I had my blood drawn earlier in the day and was now headed home from work. When I was nearly home Steph called.

"Are you on your way home?"

"Yes."

"I just got home and there's a message here from the hospital."

"What did they say?"

"You need to get home now. I need to get you to the hospital."

Heat burned up my neck. The hospital? "Why?" I asked. "What's wrong?"

"Your potassium's critically high."

"Isn't potassium a good thing?" I asked. I was nearly home by then and I didn't feel sick enough to go to the hospital. Stephanie had had issues with low potassium earlier in life and I knew that could cause a heart attack.

"Not when it's too much."

My body was fighting to clean out all the toxins from those hard-to-process foods I'd been stuffing in it. Essentially I was being poisoned. The high potassium said my kidneys were losing the battle.

My high tech filtering system was breaking down, and with it every chemical balance it controlled, including my blood pressure.

I had to see Dr. Kim the next day. I'd been the wonder kid with 43% function then. At this checkup, I was down to 21%.

"What happened?" he said. I felt terrible, like I had let him down.

I had my faith to carry me. My church was full of lots of people who loved me and prayed for me. While there, I learned to give things to Jesus, but what did that really mean?

I knew I still had control over some things, and God had control over the others, but where was the line, really? If I told him dialysis was out of the question, would God say, "Okay, no problem?"

Or was it like some people say, God is arbitrary in his healing?

Or did he sometimes put illness on a person to teach them a lesson?

I didn't have the answers to the deeper questions. What I did have was the certainty that I was NOT going on dialysis. I wasn't even going to find out about it. We were going to fix this thing.

It was as if we could again reverse the damage and buy more time. We all do that, don't we? We focus on fixing messes rather than preventing them. It is as if there is something inside of all of us that wants to test how long the tether actually is.

"Go back to what you were doing, and I'll see you in a month," Dr. Kim said.

So, I went back to controlling things. I did all the things that had worked before. I ate right. I rested. I prayed. And when I went back the next month, a chilly day in November, I had dropped down to 19%. 2% in one month.

"You need to start eating right," Doc admonished me.

"I'm trying to eat right. I'm doing what I did before."

This time it wasn't working. Everything I'd done before wasn't having the same impact. I was like the mouse at the door pushing a button but with no treat dropping out.

I was trying to sleep more, eat right, and exercise. I was doing, doing, doing, but nothing was working. My life revolved around my health and getting well.

I was in absolute denial, fed in part by the amazing recovery I'd experienced before. I had convinced myself there was no way dialysis was going to happen. I tried to control every aspect of the process. Even as I saw it happening, I couldn't accept it.

^^^^^^^^^^^^^^^^^^^^^^^^^^^^^^^^^^^^^^

"What is so bad about dialysis?" you may wonder.

Dialysis was one of my worst fears! The thought of having needles the size of a basketball air pump needle stuck in my arm at regular intervals was not appealing. How could I work if I was at dialysis three days a week for three hours a day? I'd no longer have time for all of the things that I loved to do. Staying alive would be my part-time job.

Falling into stage 5 was not part of my plan, it was not an option. Once you fall below 15% kidney function you are in stage 5. This is the final stage of the disease and is considered renal failure. At this point, it is over and I would have to get a new kidney.

^^^^^^^^^^^^^^^^^^^^^^^^^^^^^^^^^^^^^^

In December, I managed to stay at 19% kidney function. There was a glimpse of hope in the air. Could we hang on and make another comeback like before? Or, would this just be a Christmas gift of hope to get me through the holidays. Either way, I was taking it as a blessing and running with it as a torch of hope.

I am an optimist at heart and always try to look at the positive in a situation. This one was no different; I was going to continue to believe that this was not going to happen to me. I was in great physical condition and felt just fine, even though I had less energy than I once had. I ignored the flank pain in my lower back.

As if I could will it away, I kept it to myself and didn't share my symptoms with other people. I brushed off each symptom as a season change, a touch of the flu, or some other ailment. I wouldn't accept the idea that any of them were the result of my dying kidneys.

Either that, or maybe I was just that kid walking on a cold wet October night through the grave yard...whistling, and looking over his shoulder, telling himself:

"I'm not scared. I'm not scared, I'm...not...scared..."

"A champion named Goliath, who was from Gath, came out of the Philistine camp. He was over nine feet tall."

1Sa 17:4

6

Standing Face to Face with Goliath

The cold January winds sliced through the air and replaced the peace and joy of the holidays. We made our way to the end of January 2010, doing all of the things that had improved my health a couple of years prior.

Things that had once been common place took on monumental importance as I looked ahead to spring and my tenth year playing Jesus in our church's play. I looked over the script from the year before. How would I do it when I was getting weaker and making it to work was now becoming a feat?

January 28th I had my blood drawn at the lab before I went into work that morning. My numbers had been falling for months, but in the last two months they'd stabilized at 19%. Throughout the day it was hard to concentrate on work. I thought about every bite of food and every moment of activity. Was I doing it all perfectly now?

Since the numbers had stabilized for a couple of months, they could get better again. This was a turning point. There was still a chance I could control this and reverse it. It had happened once already.

The day slowly ticked away and finally I was driving my usual 50 minute drive home from Toledo, OH to Fremont, OH. I turned in to Fremont Memorial Hospital and the weight of the moment hit me: This was it.

The cold air howled into the truck the moment I opened the door. I half walked, half jogged across the lot to the front door. I grabbed the handle and pulled the door open. Warm air embraced me again and I moved down the familiar hallways to pick up the results.

Like a high school senior holding a possible college acceptance letter in my hands, I sat looking at the envelope. While it was still sealed, there remained the possibility that everything was still okay. I could even imagine things were better. Once I opened it, however, I'd realize which way my life was about to change.

Back to the icy wind. Back to the truck. I put the letter in the seat beside me. It was too much. I couldn't read it. We don't like change. Why couldn't things be the same or better? Why did something deep down seem to know that things were worse?

Ten minutes later, I was home. I turned off the ignition and sat there in the stillness of the truck. My heart raced with relentless anticipation.

Finally I began to read the results...

You know that feeling you get when the world stops for a moment, where everything freezes and it feels like you're all alone? That moment when you just know... Nothing will ever be the same after this.

This was that moment...

My kidney function had just fallen 5 percentage points down to 14% in one month. I was now officially in stage 5 of the disease. Renal failure. I was standing face to face with my Goliath. The diet that had worked miracles had not prevented the slide down. All the extra rest. Everything. I was now standing on the threshold of the realization that life as I knew it had just ended.

The papers loosened from my grip and fell to the floor as my body became numb.

It is hard to describe the feeling a person has in that moment. My truck became my cocoon. I just sat there motionless while my world was crashing down around me. My eyes stared into an abyss of an unknown future. As long as I was out here, the full reality wouldn't have to sink in. I wouldn't have to crush Stephanie's hopes like mine had been crushed.

I steeled myself and opened the door. She was waiting for the numbers.

"It's over," I said.

"What do you mean it's over?" She took the papers from my outstretched hand. She'd been strong. She was a source of strength for me. In this moment, she was afraid. I knew it. Her eyes betrayed her. She knew what these results meant as much as I did.

She scanned the sheet and I turned away. I turned away, but not before seeing hope drain from her face.

Why did I feel like such a failure? The crushing disappointment snatched hold of everything inside me. I couldn't watch the realization melt over her face, too.

I turned and stared at our barren yard through the slider doors into the backyard. There were no singing birds to comfort me. No flowers peeking out of well-manicured beds. It was the dead of winter. Everything around me was lifeless.

The world outside swirled and then cleared as I blinked back tears. Yes, in a moment like that, men cry. Forty-two is too young to face death. I wanted to comfort Stephanie. She was only 36 and facing this, too.

Stephanie's footsteps amplified and pounded in my head. I felt her arms slide around me. I was done being strong and so was she. We sobbed.

"I love you," I said.

"I love you, too."

"I don't want to do this." Another sob stole my air. I cried for a moment then continued, "I want things the way they used to be."

"It will be okay," she said.

"I'm going to have to quit everything I love doing," I sobbed. Images like a video moved in front of me, as if listing everything in life we'd now have to give up in an effort to simply survive.

I held on to Stephanie as tightly as she was holding on to me. I let my fears go. As if there was anything the poor girl could do about it.

^^^^^^^^^^^^^^^^^^^^^^^^^^^^^^^^^

We finally collected ourselves and left for our 4:40pm appointment with Dr. Kim. Now that we had the results, and had some time to work through the emotions, we were ready to see what he would suggest.

For months, Dr. Kim and I had been the yin to the other's yang. We had always balanced each other.

On the days I was pumped and ready to fight, thinking, "We can beat this!" Dr. Kim would say, "You're not doing too good."

Then, on the days when I was down, he'd reassure me, "It's not that bad, it's not that bad. You're doing really well."

We went into his office feeling the lowest we had ever felt to this point. I was certain the numbers were declaring my fate.

"Doc, it looks like I need to go on dialysis," I said.

"I don't think were quite ready for that yet," he sat confidently with my lab results beside him. Still the yin to my yang.

"You told me it takes over two months to heal up the fistula. We can't do dialysis till that's healed." I sat for a moment. Was he going to make me say it? Was this part of the acceptance process or was he still not sold on this? "In two months, I'm going to be below 5%. I won't have any percentages left."

I genuinely believe he thought that we'd seen one miracle, we could see another. We'd had that amazing jump in my numbers. He wanted to hold onto hope as much as we did.

"I've seen people go as low as 5%," he said.

"Well, all right, but what if it goes lower?" I wanted to try to hold on to that hope, too. I wasn't eager to get the fistula in.

"Well, we'd have to do an emergency port through your neck."

"I don't want to do that."

It was a tough moment for all of us. It was as if putting in the fistula would admit some kind of defeat. As if the disease had won this battle. As if there was no turning back once we did that.

"You can come back," he said. "You did it before."

We continued to talk about it for a little while, but when he saw our resolve and how upset Steph and I were, he finally made the appointment for us with Dr. Buehrer, the vascular surgeon.

Looking back it is funny; we even thought it a bit funny then. The roles had switched. Doc had more faith than we did at that moment. We'd seen one miracle the year before, Dr. Kim had hoped for two, but the peace that had flooded me two years prior was now a distant memory. A different miracle was in the works.

∧∧

That weekend, Stephanie and I did a lot of mourning and reflecting. The squeezing pain was almost unbearable. Like a bandage being wound around me tighter and tighter, the depression coiled around me until I felt like I couldn't take it any more.

Why was all of this happening to me? To us? I had done just about everything by the book. I had believed that God was going to do something awesome and turn the whole thing around. Instead, my kidneys were failing faster than they ever had. Since I'd been a Christian things had not always been perfect, but I had peace. Now I was afraid.

I thought about my family—my wife and our two girls. How would we make it if I couldn't work? Self-pity and doubt consumed me. My heart was turning bitter. Anger and confusion devoured every hope I'd held on to.

Saturday evening, I walked out back to watch the sun set over the Sandusky River. The cold icy water flowed over the dam and dropped 25 feet to the pool below. A huge orange sun hung above the horizon as the day plunged to dusk.

The wind whispered along with the sound of the water. I knelt down listening to mingling sounds and waited. I began praying. Then I waited. I listened.

I watched the sun setting and listened for God's reply. Moments from my life played in my mind and tears welled up in my eyes. Each incredible moment of victory had been a gift from God, an individual blessing.

He began to speak to me through these thoughts, reminding me that all of these blessings were preceded by trials. Those trials paved the path I was now setting out on. The thoughts soothed me. I stayed down on my knee, letting the sovereign God of the universe give me His pep talk for the upcoming battle. Not knowing just how many paths he had created that would all intersect at that one divine moment.

It's funny, when we're going through tough times we forget all of the previous trials, problems, and challenges that we have already experienced along the way. The ones that forced us to dig down deep and persevere when we didn't think we could. These larger challenges were the trials that made our previous victories even more of a blessing. Each new challenge seems insurmountable until we overcome it.

I think of David telling Saul that he had already faced previous challenges in killing a lion and a bear as they tried to run off with God's sheep. David believed God had prepared him for his epic challenge with Goliath. It seemed impossible to everyone but David. He knew God was with him and this giant was small compared to our God!

^   ^   ^   ^   ^   ^

"The Lord who delivered me from the paw of the lion and the paw of the bear will deliver me from the hand of this Philistine."   *- 1 Samuel 17:37*

As I spent the weekend facing my goliath, my donor was in his season of preparation.

What I didn't know then was that there were two other people—one I knew and one I didn't—on a collision course with my life. I couldn't see the miraculous things that were being orchestrated. I was only one player in an amazing story.

There is really no way I could have seen it at that point. I only knew I was scared and I was heading into a race against time.

I think that is true for each of us more times than we know.

7

The Preparation

I walked into my house, thinking about my encounter at the edge of the water. My mind was full of competing thoughts and ideas.

I had to start moving forward. There was planning to be done, but primarily I needed to get educated to know my enemy. Knowledge was battle armor and I was entering the war room.

We were now facing dialysis and a kidney transplant. Up to this point, we'd intentionally remained ignorant to that part of the process. We had lived with the assumption that things would never get that bad. We didn't want to know anything at all. Back then, ignorance had been our weapon.

Over the years I'd spent time reading up on my specific condition, Iga Nephropathy, but I never turned the page to find out about dialysis or transplants. Those pages were taboo. It was as if reading about that would mean I'd end up there. I had been in complete denial.

So, Stephanie and I began to search all over the internet to find out where the best hospitals were, with the best survival rates. There were so many facts and stats to consider it made our heads spin. There were survival rates, time tables, and how long it would take to get a kidney. I was completely overwhelmed.

At one point, while looking at the success rates, something occurred to me. Most of the hospitals had a 95-97% success rate. That meant I could die! I was facing life expectancy statistics. I was looking at percentages like 4% die.

You may laugh and say, "Yes, but 96% live!!" You tell that to anyone who has faced a life threatening illness and you'll likely get the same reaction from them I had—"BUT."

See, I'm a very positive person, but when you're looking at the possibility of dying—no matter how remote—it's scary. If you were in a room of people and someone said, "In two months, four of you are going to die," your mind goes to the four, not the 96.

I told that to my wife and she chuckled as I'm sure you just did when you read that. The funny thing was, at the time, I was serious. So I decided ignorance is bliss and stopped studying.

At that point we had narrowed it down to The Cleveland Clinic and Toledo University Medical Hospital (TUMC) and decided to go to bed and sleep on it.

∧∧∧∧∧∧∧∧∧∧∧∧∧∧∧∧∧∧∧∧∧∧∧∧∧∧∧∧∧∧∧∧∧∧∧∧∧∧

The next step of preparation was the most important piece to my battle plan: Bringing together an army of warriors with the most powerful weapon of all time, the power of prayer.

You see, Stephanie and I had kind of kept this phase of the disease a secret. We hadn't even told our families how bad it was. We figured if we didn't talk about it, somehow maybe it would get better.

Everyone knew I had been battling it, but they thought I was on the prednisone and everything was under control. They had no idea it was spiraling out of control the way it was. We wanted things to stay the same as much as possible and we didn't want to worry them unnecessarily.

So, on that Sunday we decided to start assembling our prayer army and telling everyone. I started by bringing in the secretary of defense and the generals, otherwise known as the pastor and the elders.

Before I could go seek them out, the pastor's wife approached me. Donna was a trustworthy and caring woman. When she approached me to ask how I was, I didn't hesitate. I poured it all out. After I had said it all, I ended with, "I want Pastor Paul and the elders to pray for me."

She didn't hesitate. After the service she was gathering a group with the battle cry, "Troy needs prayer before you leave today."

Word spread quickly as Donna told various people what was happening and others overheard. Soon there was a group of us in the front of the sanctuary. I sat on the front pew, waiting. As I sat, I started to lay out all the details. Inside my pride fought against my mouth. It is really hard for me to ask for help, even though I needed it. I felt like I was complaining. I don't like complaining. I felt a little funny about people fussing over me, but here they were.

I knew without a shadow of doubt that this was the right thing to do. I needed to put this in God's hands and with as many of God's people as possible.

So I closed my eyes and allowed the warriors to go to work.

I don't remember the context of each individual prayer. What I remember is a swirl of prayers going around me.

"Father, heal him in the name of Jesus."

"For where two or three come together in my name, there am I with them."

Matthew 18:20

In the swirl of words was the static feeling like what comes before a huge lightening storm. There was nothing really tangible that told me something was changing, but I knew something was happening. Those prayers were already being answered.

Everything was going to work out. I'd prepared myself for war by reading up on my enemy. That had only led to fear. While I sat receiving the prayers of all of these people, I was admitting my inability to do anything more and I was fully depending on God's ability. And that was freeing.

There was one prayer an elder prayed that resonated in my mind. It was almost as if he had been with me Saturday night while I struggled with my resentment and questions as I watched the sun set by the dam.

"God. Why are you allowing this to happen to a child of yours who so faithfully portrayed your son Jesus Christ in the Easter play each year?" He talked about me hanging on the cross night after night, year after year.

It was as if he was venting to God the same things that I had been. He was like a big brother shaking his fist to dad "Don't treat my little brother that way!"

The emotions crashed into each other. Faith with Fear. Trust with Confusion. The emotion of the moment churned inside me.

Then the prayer began to shift. Words of anger transformed to praise and expectation. He began to pray as if he had the same revelation I'd experienced.

"Lord you must be preparing him for something unbelievable, something so awesome and miraculous only you could do it, God. And when it's over You will be glorified through it."

The power of those words! He was saying everything I'd felt. He'd spoken of the doubts, the frustration, and the confusion. This elder had climbed into my spirit and God highlighted that single prayer to me above all others.

I hugged my army and thanked them. The buzz of prayers began to fade, but I had new peace and confidence. I absolutely knew, without a shadow of a doubt, that this would all be okay and that my prayer force was fully behind me.

^ ^ ^ ^ ^ ^ ^ ^

Having played the part of Jesus for so many years in the play, I really find it ironic the similarities with the way I came to the climax of my story and He came to the climax of His. In that the last week of Jesus' life so much is recorded. He was alive 33 years. The last three years are basically all that are talked about. Then, the last week he was on earth, there is a tremendous amount of detail. The last 72 hours are meticulously recorded.

It's the same thing here, but different.

Everything from 1992 to August 2007 when I had my 40th birthday moved along at a steady pace, with all of the normal highs and lows that one sees. Even the parts that seemed fast to me were, in retrospect, pretty mundane. Then the last three years picked up the pace and then these final six months are out of control.

Things were moving to a crescendo, and while I wasn't going to be the savior I portrayed at Easter, I was going to experience the closest thing to a resurrection I'd ever like to have.

^ ^ ^ ^ ^ ^ ^

On the way home, Stephanie had a great idea. Our friend who lived down the street, Sarah, had had a kidney transplant a little over a year prior. Why didn't we talk to her and her brother about what we were facing to find out about their experiences?

I thought this was a wonderful idea. I agreed it might help put some of our anxieties aside to actually see someone that had gone through the entire process.

Stephanie called and we spoke with them. It was a relief to hear about the process. Sarah needed a kidney and her brother Matt was a match. She told us about Dr. Rees and the process.

Hearing about the process from someone who had recently been through it made it sound so much less scary.

"Dr. Rees is the nicest doctor you could ever have. Talking to him was like talking with an old friend," she'd told us.

"I've been looking at TUMC and the Cleveland Clinic," I told her.

"Go with TUMC," she said. The confidence in her voice got me. How could she be so sure that was the right place for me? "They are close," she said. "Your loved ones can be right there and they won't have to travel far."

"I hadn't thought about that."

"Having family and loved ones visit you is very important," she said.

"That's true."

"And since TUMC is a smaller hospital, I really feel like they're able to give you more attention and make you feel like a person and not a number like some of the larger hospitals."

We agreed with that as well. We knew at that point where we wanted to go.

Thank You (Aunt) Sarah and Matt!

"Is any one of you sick? He should call the elders of the church to pray over him and anoint him with oil in the name of the Lord."   *-James 5:14*

I didn't fully appreciate the need to have people around you in tough times, until that day of prayer. I had Stephanie and my daughters, but as I had said, I didn't go beyond that. There was a huge difference when I started letting other people inside to help us.

If you or someone you know is going through difficult circumstances, the kind that shake the foundation of your soul and leave you wondering how you will ever make it through, I cannot stress enough the power of your local church and the Godly men and women inside that are there for you! These people are not the source of the power but merely an avenue to lead you to the One with the power.

When you have this kind of support group behind you as a prayer army, suddenly the impossible becomes possible and the natural becomes supernatural!!

8

On a Mission

On Monday February 1st, Stephanie called Toledo University Medical Center to get information from the nurses about starting the process. One thing about me, for better or for worse, when I make a decision to do something, I go at it with all I have. Likewise, Stephanie when she gets behind something she is committed to getting it done. We'd accepted what had to be done next, and we were charging forward.

As with most things, getting a kidney and starting dialysis would begin with a stack of forms we'd have to complete and have our Nephrologist sign. Next, those forms would be sent back to TUMC so we could be set up for the monthly kidney orientation meeting. That meeting led to an evaluation, and then finally, on the road to the waiting list for a kidney transplant.

By the end of the week, the packet of papers arrives and we started to fill out the usual forms. There are pages and pages of forms asking for everything from your middle name to your grandfather's cause of death. The questions seem endless.

Stephanie and I split up the task—she filled in all the insurance and other routine documents, while I took to filling out my family history and medical history of every known ailment that I or anyone in my family had ever had.

The packet also had a list of tests that I had to have before the transplant surgeon would even see me.

Stephanie lined up all of the appointments and they were done within a couple of weeks. The only thing left to do was have Dr. Kim fill out his part and send it into the transplant center to get us on the orientation list for the month of March.

It seemed there was an endless string of events that had to happen in a particular order to get to the next step. I had to have everything from my teeth checked to my veins mapped. I didn't even know there WAS such a thing. It almost felt like they were making up tests as a practical joke to see how many I'd do.

^   ^   ^   ^

While getting ready for a transplant, we were still prepping for dialysis but that couldn't be done until they finished vein mapping. So on February 23rd we went to take care of this hurdle.

Vein mapping is an ultrasound on your arm or area where the fistula will be located. In my case, it was my left wrist to be able to do dialysis in my forearm. This was one of the easier procedures since it didn't require any body fluids. It was also nice because the doctor came in after it was done to let me know the results.

Dr. Buehrer walked in, and greeted us with "Wow! You're my poster child here today and the youngest patient I have seen all day," he said chuckling. Most of his patients were elderly and suffered with varicose veins, carotid arteries and many other health issues that tend to hit later in life. It didn't take long to realize that Dr. Buehrer was quite the jokester.

"You have nice veins," he said. "They are large, thick and healthy."

"Thank you," I replied. He continued to turn my wrist and push on my arm periodically. He began to explain how the procedure is performed.

"An AV fistula requires advance planning because a fistula takes a while after surgery to develop—in rare cases, as long as 24 months. But a properly formed fistula is less likely than other kinds of vascular access to form clots or become infected. Also, properly formed fistulas tend to last many years—longer than any other kind of vascular access.

I will create an AV fistula by connecting an artery directly to a vein, frequently in the forearm. Connecting the artery to the vein causes more blood to flow into the vein. As a result, the vein grows larger and stronger, making repeated needle insertions for hemodialysis treatments easier. In most cases, the procedure can be performed on an outpatient basis."

After we completed our exam he scheduled the surgery for the fistula for Wednesday March 3rd.

˄   ˄   ˄   ˄   ˄   ˄   ˄

So, on March 3, 2010 my fistula surgery went off without a hitch and now it was just a matter of waiting the two and half to three months for it to heal.

On March 9th, we went to see Dr. Kim for a checkup. It had been six weeks since we had seen him. Quite a bit had happened during that time with all the tests, the surgery, and some changes I'd made in my own life.

All the changes I'd made to my diet had me feeling pretty good. My feet were a little swollen, but really, I didn't feel like a person with a terminal illness. My body didn't seem to always send me the right signals, however, so I was very curious to see where my kidney function actually was.

When we checked in, Stephanie handed the transplant documents to the receptionist.

"These are very important. Dr. Kim needs to fill them out and send them to TUMC so that we can make it to the transplant orientation later this month."

"No problem," the woman said and she took the packet away from the window. Stephanie sat next to me and we waited.

It really felt good to be back on track and know where we were going. Everything was filled out and ready. The surgery was done. The tests were completed. I was a few signatures and a meeting away from a new kidney.

The numbers weren't so good. When we met with Dr. Kim, he explained that my creatinine had risen to 6.45. That put me at 10% kidney function. That was another 4% drop.

Although it wasn't the news I wanted, I wasn't devastated. I had already accepted the fact that I was headed to a transplant, so I was prepared. I also knew everything would work out. That was why I'd spent the previous six weeks getting everything done and the fistula put in.

See, there was still a sense that I knew where I was going and how I'd get there, so it was more a challenge than a problem.

We were only two weeks from the transplant orientation meeting. All of the paper work and my testing had been completed. I had picked my brother Toby to be my donor. I was ready.

Toby had told me he would help. It had been all the way back in 2008, on a Good Friday. I had finished playing Jesus in the Easter Passion play.

"Any time, any place," he told me. "I'll be there for you. I'll be your donor." He had reminded me many times after that as well. I looked at it as God providing for me even before I had realized I'd need it.

I was so confident that this thing was on autopilot that I went into work and sat down with my boss and began to plan for my time off in July and August. Those were naturally the best times for me to recover because I'd always done well in those months. If I did it then, I reasoned, I wouldn't get sick from not having any antibodies. I was in tune with my body. I had it figured out. I'd learned the rhythm and cycle of my health, so it was obvious that getting the surgery in July would be what God wanted.

My boss didn't object, how could he? He simply asked, "Oh, he's a match?"

"Well, I'm sure he's going to be," was my confident reply. I had four brothers to choose from. I had the plan all worked out with God's help. I knew where we were going now. I was just walking it through, taking each step as it came to me. I was only waiting on the transplant meeting, the final okay, and then surgery.

At this point in the struggle God and I seemed to be on the same page. I was humming along, leaping over the hurdles as they came at me. I had the stamina to endure each new trial that rose up.

You've had those moments, right? It's like before you even say what you need, BOOM, there's the provision. Those are fun times.

I took that to mean that I finally had God's thing all figured out. I would go through the process and it would all be okay. This would work.

^   ^   ^   ^   ^   ^   ^

But then again, maybe I didn't have it all figured out...

Ten days after we saw Dr. Kim for our checkup, Stephanie realized we didn't have our invitation for the transplant orientation. She called TUMC to verify that we were on the Orientation guest list, since we had not heard back.

"I don't see you on the list," the woman said after a long pause.

"What!" Stephanie replied in shock. "What do you mean we're not on the list?" The calm was gone from her voice. "We called over a month ago and ordered the information packet," she explained. "You sent it and we filled it out and gave it to our Doctor."

She was starting to pace, agitation adding a piercing quality to her words. "I called last week and left a message with all of our information to sign up for the orientation. I don't understand."

"Can you hold for just a minute?"

Stephanie agreed. During my illness, Stephanie was my manager. There wasn't a slip of paper she couldn't locate, not a test she couldn't account for. She knew everything I'd done and would need to do.

"I want to do some more digging," the nurse said. "I'm going to keep you on hold just a bit longer while I make a couple of phone calls."

Stephanie riffled through the papers in front of her, paced, and then sat down again. I waited.

"Are you there?" the woman came back on with a friendly voice.

"Yes," Stephanie said. She returned the paper she was looking at to the neat stack in front of her and picked up a pen. Always prepared.

"The reason they never called back to confirm was they did not receive your paperwork that they were waiting on."

"But I turned them in."

"I understand. If you can get the forms to me by the end of the day, you can still get in for this month's meeting."

"I'll call you right back," she said. She clicked the phone to disconnect, then immediately dialed Dr. Kim's office.

She introduced herself quickly to the woman who answered the phone. "Has Dr. Kim signed the documents yet?"

"I put them on his desk, but let me check." There was a short pause. "It appears that Dr. Kim hasn't filled out the forms you dropped off during your appointment with him."

It was Friday. Dr. Kim was not in Fridays. They would not be able to get us in for the March orientation.

Suddenly the buzz and hum that signified that God and I were on the same page turned off. Why did this happen? How could this happen? This meant that I would have to wait until the end of April for the next meeting. I would be waiting even longer for the transplant, possibly into September. That 4% plunge that hadn't really worried me ten days ago was now suddenly huge.

Everything had been going as planned and now this! We had done everything in record time and as efficiently as possible. The helplessness of knowing those forms were just going to sit there was almost more than I could bear. I wanted to take control again. I'd gone from peace and trust to anger and frustration.

^   ^   ^

It took some time but we finally let go of our anger. After we cooled off, we realized we had done everything humanly possible to make it happen. It was a hard pill to swallow. In our helplessness—and resignation—we came to the place where all we could say was, "God must not have wanted us to go to the March orientation for some reason."

"Trust in the Lord with all your heart and lean not on your own understanding; in all your ways acknowledge him, and he will make your paths straight." –Proverbs 3:5-6

9

Seeds Along the Path

The next four weeks trickled by like sand in an hourglass. We wished each day away, while still clinging to the value of each one. It felt like such a waste of time to see four weeks drift past and there was not a thing we could do to speed things up. All of the testing was complete and we had all the paper work in. My brother Toby was waiting to see when he would have to do his testing. There was absolutely nothing left to be done but wait.

One thing I could do was control my own habits. I continued to be very strict with my diet and lifestyle as I waited for the big week to come. Despite my diligence, the only change in my health was increased fatigue and swelling feet. Not encouraging, but also not tragic.

Friday, April 16th I had my blood work done for my appointment with Dr. Kim the following Tuesday. That afternoon I again picked up the results from the Fremont Memorial Hospital. My creatinine had climbed to 8.6. My kidney function had dropped to 7%!

It was like I had no control over my body at all. No matter what I did, things got worse. I couldn't even trust my body for signals. I felt pretty good for the most part; I was still watching everything that I was doing but nothing I did mattered.

I made the trip home again. I had given up trying to explain these things anymore.

"I'm at 7%," I said to Stephanie when I walked in the door.

For a moment her expression was her only reply. She looked at me. Dumbfounded. "Wow," she finally said. It was part word, part exasperated exhale. It articulated what we both knew. Time was running out.

I needed the Elders to pray again. The coming week was so full of appointments it would make up for the four week lull we'd endured. We would visit the dialysis unit, see Dr. Buehrer, Dr. Kim, and finally go to the transplant orientation.

^   ^   ^   ^   ^   ^   ^

Sunday morning, I explained the situation to Pastor Paul and the elders. "My kidneys are at about 7% of normal function and they're failing fast." Saying it made it even more real. The words had new sting. But it was this group of prayer warriors who had renewed my spirit before through their prayers. I knew they cared about me. I knew they could pray me through again. "I need to go on dialysis before my kidneys fail completely."

"We will pray now." They began to gather around me.

"I also need you to pray for the orientation," I said. The feeling of God's presence was already building. "Pray this thing moves along quickly."

So they prayed…

And God showed up.

It was another awesome moment like I'd experienced a couple of months ago. I don't mean awesome as in really neat. This was awe inspiring. I knew God was going to continue doing something amazing.

^   ^   ^   ^   ^   ^   ^

Monday evening, Stephanie and I were talking about what dialysis might be like. We'd continued to take things as they came. Even though my sister-in-law Debbie worked at a dialysis center 10 minutes away, I'd not asked her about it. Remember my ignorance-is-bliss theory. Unfortunately, that was no longer possible.

I had already decided that I didn't want dialysis to interfere with work. While going through a major illness, you fiercely guard any remaining pieces of normalcy. I was still feeling pretty good for the most part and I still felt a need to provide for my family.

"I'd rather go two hours a day, twice a week," I told her. Then, I decided to call Debbie. Toby answered, and after usual pleasantries, passed the phone to Debbie.

We talked for a little bit but it was pretty clear that my hopes of doing dialysis for small amounts of time were not going to happen.

"And Troy, we're filled to capacity right now. The nearest open unit will probably be up in Toledo," Debbie said. An hour trip to each treatment had not been a part of my plan.

"Is there any way you could talk to someone?" I asked.

"I'll see what I can do, but I'm not sure," Debbie told me. "Would you like to come over tomorrow and see the dialysis unit and how it works?"

"Sure, we'll come over after our appointment with Dr. Buehrer and Dr. Kim."

It was starting to look like, once again, that I wasn't in control of this thing.

Λ   Λ   Λ   Λ   Λ   Λ

The next day, Tuesday, April 20, we went to see Dr. Buehrer. We hoped that by some small miracle he would say the fistula was ready and that I could start dialysis. My symptoms were now starting to show. I was tired and run down. Hopefully with dialysis I'd start to feel more energy.

He walked in and checked it. "It is looking good." He moved my wrist around a bit, "It's healing really well. The surgeon must have done an amazing job."

We laughed, because, of course, he was that guy. The levity was enough to make me feel pretty good.

"Well, you ought to be ready to go next month," he said. His voice was confident and light, as if delivering great news to me.

"Not now, huh?" I said, my voice pleading.

"Why, what's wrong?"

The levity of the moment now gone, he looked at me. My body was a liar, though. As I'd said earlier, to look at me I seemed fine, but with 7% kidney function, I really didn't have a month to spare. My energy was nearly gone, and I was starting to have a hard time getting through the day.

"I'm at 7%," I said.

"Really! 7%. You would never know it by looking at you," he looked again at the scar and felt the buzzing of the fistula.

For those that don't know what that is, it is the vibration felt through the skin from the blood flowing through the artery into the vein. It feels like there is a little motor running or maybe some crickets under your skin chirping away. It reminded one little girl of her kitty, when it purrs.

Dr. Buehrer continued to inspect my arm, squeezing in different areas. His examination had changed in urgency. It seemed he was trying to find a reason to tell me the fistula wasn't ready. Finally, he looked at me.

"I don't see any reason why we can't start now. Your veins are so good; I believe we can get away with it."

The buzzing in my ears stopped. I took a deep breath. God had come through again. We didn't have to wait another month.

~ 83 ~

With this hurdle crossed, we were one appointment away from what we hoped would be our next miracle, a spot at dialysis and then a return to feeling good again.

^   ^   ^

We left there and went straight to Dr. Kim's office to share the news with him. He seemed just as relieved as we were. Next came deciding where I'd have dialysis.

"Fremont's dialysis center is at capacity," he began. Of course, I knew that from Debbie. "I'm not affiliated with them so I'm not able to get you in there," he continued. "They have about 60 patients there and only three of them are mine."

We'd have to look at going to Toledo or another city. He began to explain some of the centers and our options.

"Well," I began, "My sister-in-law, Debbie, works there. We're actually going over there for a tour after we leave here."

"Can she get you in there?"

The question struck us as a bit odd. We laughed. Dr. Kim was asking *us* if my sister-in-law could get us in. Wasn't that his job? We found out later he was a little intimidated by Debbie's boss, Deb. However, he did put in a phone call while we were on our way back to Fremont.

^   ^   ^

When we arrived at the dialysis center for our orientation, my sister-in-law Debbie and her boss Deb were standing at the door. We got out of our car and made the awkward walk up the sidewalk that a person makes when they are being watched.

Debbie is a very soft spoken person with a very reserved personality. She is a lovely lady. Contrast that to her boss, Deb. Deb stood there, all five foot of her, skinny as a rail and full of fire and spunk—just like I'd imagined. I couldn't wait to meet her after hearing that Dr. Kim was intimidated by her.

We were nearly to the doors now. I smiled and got ready to say hello when Deb started.

"Look here buddy," she stared me dead in the eye as she spoke. "I can get you in but it's only going to be for two days a week and for two hours a day and that's it! We just don't have any openings."

I looked at Stephanie and we both started laughing. "That will work just fine," I said.

I explained that I wanted those exact hours and that what she was offering was exactly what I'd prayed for.

She listened and then said, "Well, we can start you this coming Monday." Less than a week, wow!

So they showed us around and explained how the whole process operates. It turned out Deb was actually a big sweet heart.

We went home that night knowing God had just answered more prayers. Everything was just coming together. The next night was the kidney coordination meeting we had been waiting for. I had been like a kid waiting for Christmas.

∧∧∧∧∧∧∧∧∧∧∧∧∧∧∧∧∧∧∧∧∧∧∧∧∧∧∧∧∧∧∧∧∧∧∧∧∧∧∧

"In his heart a man plans his course, but the Lord determines his steps."   *- Proverbs 16:9*

When I look back over the pieces that fell in to place, it is easy to see the major miracles, but what about the other things that lined up. Like my sister-in-law who went to nursing school later in life. She graduated only about ten years before I would need dialysis.

Around that same time, a dialysis unit built an office here in Fremont and she took a job there. At that time, we had no idea I'd ever need that. She was working there each day, never realizing the critical role she was going to play in my life. Not knowing that I was going to need her.

But God did. He was preparing the way for me.

Look around in your own life and I am sure you will see these small predestined miracles. The ones that make people say "well isn't that ironic" or "what a coincidence".

These are God's seeds that he leaves along the path of life. Signs to let you know, He is in front of you guiding the way. Even when you think things are out of control, He shows you He's in complete control.

10

Nurses or Angels

Wednesday, April 21, the day of the kidney orientation meeting, we were ready. Stephanie had organized all of my information. From the application to the testing and blood work of the last two years in a folder, each and every piece of information from the packet was completed. While we'd learned there were things we could not control, we also had learned the best way to take the upper hand in a situation was to be prepared.

We walked into the education wing of the hospital and walked down the hallway to a classroom. Have you ever seen the movies that show these large lecture halls with stadium seating? That was this room. The size of it alone was intimidating. Then, I looked around the room. There had to be about 60 people there to get a transplant. These were held month after month.

My resolve wavered briefly. Simple math said at this hospital alone there were dozens of people going on the transplant list every month. Would I even get my kidney in time?

We went ahead and signed in and took the information they gave us. We found a seat and started to sift through the stack of papers.

I looked around the room. Each person there was a story. Why were they getting a transplant? How long had they suffered with their condition? What brought them to this point? Was their illness sudden like mine or had they been battling their whole lives?

There were people of every age and nationality, people younger than me, maybe in their 20s or 30s, all the way up to people who were clearly pushing 70. Disease isn't prejudiced. Each of these people, like me, had organs that were failing. And each of these people had someone there supporting them like I did. A disease like this is not something that you can do alone.

Two women stood at the bottom of the classroom. I'd later learn that these were two nurses, Amy and Sandy.

"Okay, we're going to begin now," Amy said.

"Please pull out the information you were given when you came in. We will be going through all of this with you tonight."

First, there was the financial cost. Even without counting the cost of a transplant, the annual cost of immunosuppressant drugs is $41,000. "You will need to be able to cover this cost or you will not be put on the transplant list." These drugs would keep you alive by preventing rejection. "There are insurances and programs that will assist you in covering most of this cost."

That was only half of the equation. We were told that any living donors would be covered 100% by Medicare. So, there would be virtually no cost to the donor for this courageous act of generosity.

"Once we have you on the list," she continued, "We must have good phone numbers where we can reach you 24/7 in the event that a cadaver kidney becomes available."

We would need to make a decision on the spot whether to accept or reject a kidney. Why would we reject one? Some kidneys come from people with all sorts of questionable life styles—you may not want that particular one.

They covered the testing procedure for the live donors. The live donors would have to be completely healthy with a low body mass index. They could not have high blood pressure or smoke. The list went on and on. In some cases they would have to go through more testing than the recipient to insure they were a good prospect. The health of the live donor was as important, if not more important, than that of the recipient.

The meeting continued into the second hour with information on the testing procedure, surgery, and post-op. They did a great job explaining things.

"Does anyone have any questions?" Amy asked.

People began to ask a variety of questions. Some were very practical about the procedure. Others were ridiculous, like one about artificial kidneys.

"When will they be coming out with an artificial kidney?"

Amy and Sandy exchanged a confused glance.

"Your gonna have to ask someone smarter than us that question," Amy answered. We laughed but these questions were just a waste of our time. There was really only one question that was relevant and no one else seemed to be asking it.

I looked around and no one had their hand raised, so I raised mine.

Amy looked at me, "Yes?"

"When do we get started?" I asked.

"We will call you," Amy replied and scanned the room, I assumed, to see if there were any other questions. That wasn't an answer. I raised my hand again. She pointed at me.

"When?" I asked. "Like in a couple of weeks?"

"Oh, heavens no!" She was kind, but it was obvious by her voice that I'd asked a ridiculous question. "It could be five months. You see all of these people in here?" She motioned to the room with a sweep of her hand.

I shot back, "But I have all of my testing done and I have a list of donors. I'm ready to go!"

Amy and Sandy looked at each other for a moment and then back at me.

"We will call you," they said. Their voices were softer than before.

I felt like I was raising my hand like Horse Shack from "Welcome back Kotter". (That's dating myself.) Why continue? They'd give the same answer.

Stephanie started to raise her hand. I grabbed her arm. "No, I have an idea," I whispered.

We waited a few minutes for the questions to stop and the meeting to end. Amy and Sandy dismissed the group and people started to file out. Stephanie stood up and started to turn toward the exit.

"Sit down," I took her hand and guided her back beside me. "I'm going to try talking to the nurses."

She sat down but her expression said, "Yeah right. They already told you five months."

It didn't hurt to try but I wanted to be sure everyone was out of the room. If there was any chance something else could be done, I had to wait until everyone was gone.

When the last of the people were filing out of the door at the back of the room, Stephanie and I walked down the steps to the bottom where Amy and Sandy were sitting and going over papers.

I called Sandy over by me. When she came, I opened my folder and said, "Sandy, here's the deal. I have all of my testing done and completed. I have a list of donors that are interested in donating. My kidney function is all the way down to 7% and I haven't started dialysis yet."

"Really, you haven't even started dialysis yet? You have ALL of your testing done?" She started to look at my folder.

"Yes, and I have donors, too." Sandy turned and looked back at Amy.

"It's really unusual to see someone show up with everything already done and ready to go," Sandy started. "Usually people drag their feet to get all of the testing done." She continued to look through my information as she spoke and a couple of times looked up at Amy.

"Really?" I asked. That was perplexing to me. We are talking about life and death. I cannot imagine not doing whatever was necessary to stay alive.

Sandy pointed to a number and looked at Stephanie, "Call this number tomorrow and talk to this lady. Tell her that I told you to call and that you will bake her some cookies. She will work you into the schedule."

Our faces must have been beaming with joy and disbelief. It seemed awfully funny to call with the promise of cookies. I honestly don't think they made the difference between getting an organ or not, but it was a funny comment that helped lighten the mood.

Stephanie started to scribble down everything Sandy was saying. We were not going to have to wait five months after all. The room brightened. Again, our preparation had paid off.

"What's going on?" Amy asked. Sandy started to tell her what she'd just told us.

"No, no we can't do that," Amy said with a stern look on her face. Our excitement began melting to disappointment. I didn't need a mirror to see it. We'd almost made it. Fear and dread now replaced the positive. So close and then only to have it jerked away.

Amy continued, "Here is what we're going to do. I am going to talk to Dr. Rees tomorrow. We will call you in a couple of days to schedule an appointment for you. We should be able to get you in next week."

My mouth fell to the floor, I was speechless. Not expecting that to come out of her mouth, I was blown away. This was even easier than Sandy's plan. Amy was going straight to the doctor. Wow!

"Okaaayyy," was all that I could get out. It was no longer the excitement of the possibility. This was now really real. The doctor. The transplant. It could still happen on my timeline.

"You know, we were supposed to be here last month," Stephanie began. "The application sat on our doctor's desk two days too long." She put her pen in her bag and looked between Sandy and Amy.

"If we would have been here last month we might be getting a transplant even sooner."

Amy and Sandy glanced at each other with smirks and let Stephanie finish venting. It wasn't that we were ungrateful, but we'd been ready for a month. It had been a month of unnecessary delay.

Amy responded, "If you would have come last month you would not have had us. You would have had a couple of nurses filling in for us. They wouldn't have been able to get you in like this. I'm the head kidney transplant coordinator and Sandy is in charge of the patients, post-operation."

Neither of us spoke at that moment, but once again we were humbled by the incredible way this had played out. We finished our conversation and made our way to the van.

We got in, and together stared out the window, as to stare into the abyss. We both had these surreal grins on our faces, as we slowly started to exhale expressions of "huh" and "wow". Our minds went to those earlier thoughts of "Well, I guess God had other plans."

Then, we began to chuckle in disbelief.

"Did that just happen?" I said as Stephanie looked at me and said "I love you."

We hugged. Then, started the engine and pulled away as we laughed and cried, realizing something incredible had just happened.

^   ^   ^   ^

It is amazing when we look back on various occasions in life—when you first meet people—not realizing the full impact that person will have on your life. This is when people come in to your life that have your best interest in mind and want victory as bad as you do. You may not realize it at the moment, but in retrospect you can't help but wonder if they were put there for a reason.

This was one of those moments and Amy and Sandy were two of those people. From that day on, Stephanie would refer to Amy as our guardian angel and after the surgery, Sandy would take the reins over.

^^^

"For he will command his angels concerning you to guard you in all your ways"

- Psalms 91:11

11

Love it When a Plan Comes Together

A couple of days later, Amy called to let us know the appointment was scheduled for the following Thursday (April 29th) at 1:15. Things were really moving along. It was exciting.

"Bring up to three donors to be tested and be prepared to be there the rest of the day."

I was sure I'd only need my brother Toby. I called him and let him know when the appointment was, so he could get the day off work.

I was also about to start dialysis. My first appointment would be April 26th. With everything lining up so well, I didn't figure I'd have to go there too many times and then this chapter would be behind us. Things were finally going to be back to normal. I could see clearly what was on the horizon, something that gave me a good deal of comfort.

^   ^   ^   ^   ^   ^   ^

On Monday, Stephanie and I went to the dialysis center at 4:30 in the afternoon to begin dialysis treatments. The first and last thing they do when you are going through dialysis is weigh you. (When I arrived I weighed 180 lbs). This helps them determine how much fluid they needed to pull off and then, see how much they actually took.

One odd thing I learned was since most everyone in there has been on dialysis for quite some time, they have stopped urinating all together. Dialysis is how fluids and toxins are removed from the body. Since I was a newbie, I was one of the few people who still used the bathroom.

After they weighed me, they sent me to a lazy boy chair to sit down and get comfortable. They hooked me to an automatic blood pressure cuff and checked my blood pressure a couple of times. 144/93 seemed to be average at that time. As the nurse began to prepare all of the hoses and the needles, I began to draw a crowd.

The staff knew that I was the new kid and Debbie's brother-in-law, so I seemed to draw an unusual amount of interest.

Three nurses stood in front of me, alternating between glances at me and then my numbers. They had something like a coy smirk. It was similar to that of an older sister who understands something her little brother doesn't.

Finally I couldn't take it anymore, and smiling I said, "What!?"

A woman I later learned was named Heather said, "We are looking at your numbers and we are looking at you. We know that you are still going to work and getting around. By the look of these numbers, you should look a lot worse than you do and be in a bed somewhere."

~ 98 ~

I just smiled.

Stephanie immediately seized the opening to tell them about the journey we had experienced so far and how we continued to beat the odds—even with the disease's progression.

I felt the pinch in my forearm as the first of two needles were inserted. It was a feeling I'd grown accustomed to with all the blood work. The first treatment went pretty well. Dialysis treatments would be a breeze—after the needle. I didn't think this was going to be all that bad, which was welcomed relief. I'd only have to endure this twice a week for the next couple of months until I'd have my life back again.

^   ^   ^   ^   ^   ^   ^   ^

The meeting with Dr. Rees was only a couple of days away. With the panic subsiding, I had an opportunity to think about my brother, Toby, and the courageous act of love he was preparing for.

I had to go through this surgery to survive, but he was excited to be able to donate his kidney to his little brother. I was so sure this was what God was directing since this whole path had been so smooth for the most part. His wife working at the dialysis center and helping me get in. Toby himself wanting to donate—it seemed as if it was meant to be.

That's why when my older brother Tony called me up that evening, clear out of the blue, I was so surprised. It had been months since we'd last spoke. It's not that we didn't get along; it's just that we weren't a chatty family. Plus, Tony lived

2½ hours away up in Chesaning, Michigan. He had also been an ordained Pastor for years and moved around from time to time.

"Troy. What do I have to do to get tested?" Tony's voice was nonchalant. It was no tenser than as if he'd called to tell me about a gathering.

"Tony, you don't have to do that. Toby already is getting tested and he'll be a match," I said with the confidence born of a man who has God's cell phone number. I didn't feel it was necessary for him to make the two and a half hour trip down from Michigan to Toledo, just to help me, when I knew Toby was going to be a match.

"Yeah, well, I think you're going to need me."

We went back and forth for just a little bit, with Tony's persistence winning out. He seemed so set on doing this that I figured, the more the merrier.

"I appreciate that," I said, "Show up on Thursday and we will all get tested."

When I got off the phone, I was just dumbfounded for a moment. What were the odds that he'd call just two days before the appointment and ask to get tested. Huh.

^   ^   ^   ^   ^   ^   ^   ^

On Thursday, April 29th, we all met at TUMC. We made our way up to the transplant center and waited for our appointment. Once they called our names, Toby and Tony were sent to have 12 – 15 tubes of blood drawn. Then, they met with a coordinator and were briefed on the donor process much like I had been in my transplant meeting earlier that month.

The coordinator paints a very graphic picture of the process and the pain and risks involved. They told them there is a 1 in 3000 chance you could die during the surgery—due to unforeseen complications—and so on and so on. When their meeting ended, I was still going through all of my testing so they left.

My meeting started out a little different than my brothers'. Stephanie and I met with Amy, who would be our kidney coordinator, and Sandy, who would be our nurse. They briefed us on the process and then, we began to fill out forms. After a while of that, we waited for the next set of coordinators to come in.

Our financial coordinator and the psychological coordinator walked in next. For the financial coordinator, we filled out forms to determine what types of financial aid and other programs we might qualify for.

You'll recall, these drugs that would keep me alive after the transplant cost more than some of us make in an entire year. She did such a great job of explaining things to us. It wasn't until afterwards that we realized how valuable her work was. Many of our drug expenses were 100% covered by different programs she signed us up for.

Then, the psych exam and all of the questions they needed answered. I was asked about everything from my childhood to my family. They ask you all kinds of personal questions, trying to find out if you're stable or not. I didn't quite understand why a recipient would have to go through this exam. Thankfully, I passed it.

"Troy, can you come with me?" a woman said.

Stephanie stayed in the office waiting for Dr. Rees, while I followed the woman down the hall to have my blood drawn.

ᴧ   ᴧ   ᴧ

I was looking forward to meeting Dr. Rees. I had heard so many good things about him from Sarah our neighbor. He had a reputation for being a friendly guy, so as I walked back to the transplant wing, I had a big ole smile on my face.

I walked in the door and was immediately struck by how grim things were in the room. Dr. Rees turned to me, stuck his hand out to shake mine and said in voice that was more condolence than greeting, "I'm Dr. Rees, I'm sorry you have to go through this."

The smile slowly slid from my face and my mood dropped to reach the mood of the room. I shifted my gaze to Stephanie then back to Dr. Rees.

"That's alright, it's not your fault," I said, trying to lighten the mood. I looked over at Stephanie again. Her expression mirrored mine. *What the heck?*

He didn't smile; he just sat down and began to ask some questions. After the last question, Doc and Amy left the room.

I looked over at Stephanie and said, "He must be having a bad day." Where was this super sweet man we had heard all about? You know, the one that seems like he's known you for years. Instead, the Dr. Rees we'd met that day seemed grumpy and like he didn't want to be there with us.

"Ya think!" she replied not even trying to mask the sarcasm. I laughed and waited for them to return.

When Doc returned, he asked Stephanie to step out while he gave me an exam.

The Dr. Rees that came back in the room was totally different. He told me about the process and how the surgery worked. I told him about the path that had led me to needing a kidney transplant.

Next, he looked me over and checked many of my vitals. He poked me in different spots to insure my health was good. Next, he sat down at his computer and pulled up the complete medical history I had filled out.

He flipped through a series of pages with numbers, graphs, x-rays, and words. Everything I'd lived medically over the past decades, summarized in a list of numbers.

He turned around in his chair, looked at me and said, "I have done over 300 transplants and you could potentially be the healthiest patient that I have ever seen. You have not had any illnesses, surgeries, broken bones, or anything else wrong with you. You just have a kidney disease; there is nothing else wrong with you."

Seemed like an odd statement to make. I thought the kidney thing was enough of an illness, but what I later came to realize was Dr. Rees was used to seeing patients with diabetes and all kinds of other ailments that led to their kidneys failing.

I just had this rare kidney disease that only affected the kidneys. I figured that was a good thing, so that bit of trivia really made me feel good.

"Do you have any questions?" he asked.

I thought for a moment. I could only think of one that mattered much at that point. I smiled and said, "What are the success statistics on your surgeries?"

He smiled and told me a bit about the 300 surgeries. While he'd really lost very few patients, it was clear in his voice that those losses were very personal to him. One of them in particular, was with someone who'd had a weakened artery he could never have seen.

"Wow," I said. How hard must it have been to lose someone to something like that? I had been facing my own mortality over these last couple of years, but I knew my enemy was the kidney disease. What must it have been like to have your own artery turn against you just as you were getting ready to have a new life?

The other person he'd lost had been even more tragic in my eyes. The man had committed suicide months after the surgery.

"And he was doing great too!" Doc said with a stern voice of disgust.

~ 104 ~

That explained the psych coordinator.

"But, those are the exceptions," he continued. Then, he talked about the success stories. He reassured me that he is very good at what he does.

He talked about the experimental projects he was in charge of and the strides forward they were making. He talked very highly of the transplant team and assured me I would be well taken care of.

^^

When we left that afternoon, I knew without a shadow of a doubt I had made the right choice. Dr. Rees was a man of obvious compassion who could be trusted.

Everything was coming together so nicely. I could already see this happening in July as I had planned. It might even be sooner at the current rate.

I saw the story of perseverance and faith unfolding. I had this thing all figured out. I knew God was in control of my plan, the plan I had.

^^

"Many are the plans in a man's heart, but it is the LORD's purpose that prevails"

- ***Proverbs 19:21***

12

God Chuckles

Now it was a waiting game. For the next two weeks, we waited for my brothers' results. To me, it was nothing more than a formality. One of my brothers was going to be a match. Then, I was going to have surgery and move on. It was just a matter of going through the process.

This is the way it works. A transplant team examines the donor's test results and then contacts the donor to let them know. If the donor has changed their mind, the transplant team cannot tell the recipient. If the donor wants to continue to go through the process—and is a match—they can let the transplant team know, as well as the recipient.

The first week went along like normal, but the second week seemed painfully slow. By the middle of week two, Stephanie started calling Amy daily to check for updates.

In the late afternoon of Thursday, May 13th, I was at work when I received a phone call from my brother up in Michigan, Tony. I was in my office when the call came in and I walked outside for privacy.

I had the nervous pulse of a man with his life on the line. I was as anxious as each time I'd opened my blood labs.

"Well little brother, I'm not a match," he said. His voice was a mixture of disappointment and concern. My heart shot up to my throat for a moment. I had just lost my backup plan.

"You are kidding me?" I said with deep concern in my voice.

"I had the CMV virus at some point in my life and you haven't, so they won't use me."

We talked for a little while longer. His voice told me how disappointed he was with the outcome. I was, too. My faith teetered slightly, but I still had Toby. Toby was the one who was going to be my donor any way. It'd been planned.

"Thanks for coming all the way down here to get tested," I said.

"No problem."

We said our goodbyes and hung up.

I remained outside staring at nothing in particular for quite a while. Pieces of conversations I'd had came in and out of my mind as I stood thinking. Doc had said I was one of the healthiest patients he'd ever had. While that was normally good, it also meant I had not had this virus. I was one of a very few who'd never had this virus. I was always one of the exceptions. I had no idea what that meant for my chances, now. My good health could cost me my life. Talk about irony.

Finally, I walked out, got in my truck and began driving home. Then, I called home.

Stephanie answered.

"I've got some news," I said. Then I explained the latest. She was as disappointed as I was but continued to build optimism and hope that Toby was still my guy.

"You've been saying that Toby was your guy all along. Don't worry."

By the time I pulled in my driveway, Stephanie had me believing again. The fear and disappointment was washed away and I focused on talking to Toby to see when we could get rolling on things.

I waited until 4:30 and called Toby. I got no answer.

Well, he usually got home around 4 or 4:30, so I called again 15 minutes later. No answer.

I called again at 5 and still no answer. This time I left a message. "Hey Toby, Tony just got his results a little while ago. Yours should be ready too."

Less than an hour later, the phone rang. It was Toby. I walked to our bedroom and shut the door.

"Hey," he started. "I just got off the phone with the transplant center." His voice was very calm and steady. I couldn't get a read on it.

"Yeah?" I said, my voice the opposite of his cool composure.

"They told me that I am a near perfect match, but they can't use me." My pulse began to race. He continued, "I had a kidney stone *7 years ago* and because of that they won't do it."

My stomach and my heart fought to climb into my throat. The disappointment was so intense I thought I was going to vomit. My limbs grew weaker and weaker as all of my hopes and aspirations were jerked out from under me like a rug. The phone turned to lead in my hand and I lie back on my pillows as he continued to tell me what the transplant team had said.

"How could this be?" I said.

"I don't know." Toby tried to make sense of it. He summarized the questions he'd asked the transplant team and the ways he'd tried to get around what seemed to be an unreasonable formality.

After all, it had been 7 YEARS AGO. But the team made it clear it was not up for debate; they were not going to use him.

"I'll keep trying and ask more questions. Maybe they will change their mind," he said.

He was just trying to cheer me up.

I hung up the phone and let my shoulders drop. My mind drifted. It felt like the world had stopped again. I was like Atlas holding the weight of the world up on my shoulders. Again, I'd have to tell Stephanie that things were unknown. Tears pooled in my eyes but didn't fall. Everything was in suspended animation. I was so weak.

I stayed there, hunched, leaning forward with my arms dangling. That is how Stephanie found me when she walked in the bedroom a few minutes later.

She stopped in front of me and silently placed her hands on my shoulders.

"What just happened?" I gasped. "What are we gonna do?"

The tears broke their barrier and poured down my face. I looked up and saw she'd beaten me there. Her crying was only superseded by my loud, convulsive cries. The sobs rocked my body until I was nearly hyperventilating.

It is nearly impossible to describe the pain. I was devastated, destroyed, crushed, defeated, broken, and beaten. I felt helpless and abandoned.

I felt hopeless...

The closest emotion I'd felt before that time, or since, was the depression that comes with mourning a loved one's death.

In my case, the mourning was not over someone but over something. It was hope. The hope I'd felt at the prospect of my transplant and starting to live again by July was now over.

The assurance of knowing that one of my brothers would be a donor was officially over. I would never have that feeling of security again to fall back on.

I felt like David standing in front of Goliath with no stone in the sling and none in the pouch.

How it is possible that I have four brothers and none would be able to help me? That confident faith born of absolutely knowing how it would work out? It was now replaced by a pile of questions and fear.

Why was this happening?

God and I seemed to be on the same page all along. It was so obvious the way he had been working everything out.

The fistula healing in half the time, getting into dialysis in Fremont and for two hours on two days, the coordination meeting and getting into see Dr. Rees in a week instead of five months. Everything had been falling into place.

That plan I believed was working out just the way I wanted it to, had vanished. My hope had been rooted in understanding it would all be okay.

Why? Why would God do this? Why would he just pull the rug out from underneath me? Where was he going with this? The vision I had seen was over. I had no idea what the future held and that scared me more than I can articulate.

The safety net I had was gone!

^^^^^^^^^^^^^^^^^^^^^^^^^^^^^^^^^^^^^

"For my thoughts are not your thoughts, neither are your ways my ways," declares the Lord.

"As the heavens are higher than the earth, so are my ways higher than your ways and my thoughts than your thoughts"   *- Isaiah 55:8-9*

You see, I had been seeing this story as something I could comprehend. It was very possible. It's my story with a plan I'm devising and making happen with God's help. It allowed me to be in control and in a kind of comfort zone. I could see the ending and just needed God to work it out. It made it easy for me to go around praising God for all the cool stuff He was doing—since I knew there was going to be a happy ending, or so it seemed.

I believe God has a sense of humor. I believe it was probably at this point, God chuckled and said "Cute story son, now sit down and hang on for the ride! Let me show you a real story. You might not like it while you're going through it, but you will when it's over."

I believe God said this through my brother Toby. By the fluky way he was rejected and the fact that it was seven years ago—seven being one of the most famous bible numbers— acted as God's fingerprint. It was a statement to make sure I knew He was in charge. If that wasn't enough, God would say

"Oh yeah, you were right, Toby would end up being the best match of anyone ever tested! But that isn't my plan!"

It's easy to believe when you know you're not going to sink. But try stepping out of the boat when you can't see the bottom.

The safety nets are gone; there is no backup plan. You are walking on faith alone. Though we felt abandoned and hopeless, we knew...

Hope was really all we had left at this point...

13

Truck Driver or Messenger of Hope

In retrospect, I can see God's hand but at the time I was depressed by this setback. The only thing I knew I could do was put more prayer warriors on the battlefield and start getting the word out that I needed a donor.

When I went to church that Sunday, I asked some people to pray with me after church. We prayed God would give us comfort, as well as find me a donor.

^   ^   ^   ^

The week after I found out my brothers were not matches, God sent an angel in the form of a truck driver. This guy was probably about 60 and kind of looked like a leprechaun. He was about 5'4", 5'5" with a big, square, pudgy face that held a permanent smile. He was stocky and talkative—in fact, he talked out of one side of his mouth.

I'd never seen him in my life and I've worked for the company for 20 years. I know many of the truck drivers from seeing them on job sites.

On this particular day I was feeling pretty low. He came walking in with a gait that was part waddle, part limp, and said, "Hey, I've got some pipe out here for ya."

"Oh, okay."

Now, at this time it was about May. I wasn't doing too well because we had just started dialysis and my kidney function was down to 5%. I was battling fatigue and discouragement.

We were unloading the truck and he said, "Oh, man, I probably shouldn't be doing this because my back hurts."

"Really," I said.

"Yeah."

I looked at the pile slowly moving from the truck to our building—we were each only carrying one piece at a time—and I said, "I probably shouldn't be doing it either."

"Oh yeah? Why?"

"I've got a kidney disease, I'm on dialysis and I'm not doing too well." I put the pipe on the pile and started back to the truck to get the next one. "But I'm all right," I added.

"Really?"

At that moment he stopped carrying pipe and started talking to me.

I bet we stood there for a half hour or better. He was in no hurry—almost as if he was putting my concerns above all.

"You guys are a bunch of good guys," he said. "I just started this week, but I like this company."

"Really? This is your first week?"

"Yep. This is my first trip." He extended his hand to me. "My name's Larry. It's nice to meet you."

I took his hand. "Yeah. You, too."

He started sharing with me how he came to be hired with the company. Somewhere along the line, he started talking about God and church.

"You're a Christian, aren't you?" he said.

"Yes."

"I knew you were, I could just tell."

He was a funny guy. It's almost like he could sense things. We sat there on that unusually warm day with the garage door open, the only two people around.

Off in the background, you could hear the buzzing of traffic, but there we were talking and unloading the truck, then talking some more.

I told him my brothers weren't a match and the disappointment with it. He was easy to talk to, so I talked to him.

"You know," he said, "I know your brothers aren't a match and everything, but I have a feeling this is all going to work out for you."

I wanted to believe it, but I wasn't sure, so I didn't respond.

~ 117 ~

"Don't tell me what it is," he continued, "but I just got a feeling God's got something special for you."

I sat there smiling and nodding my head. He'd been there for a while and we had carried all of the pipe in.

"Before I leave, I'd like to pray with you," he said.

Nobody does that on a construction site. I was shocked and comforted.

"Alright."

We talked a couple more minutes. Then, he stuck his hand out and I shook his hand. In that moment, he grabbed me by the hand and shoulder and started to pray.

It was unbelievable. For about five minutes, he prayed strong prayers. I did nothing but listen to him and let the prayers wash over me.

"Amen," he said and I opened my eyes. He had a big grin on his face. He winked and waddled back to his truck, got in and drove away. I watched him go, thinking, "Did that just happen?" I've never experienced that before. Not in this place. I couldn't help but wonder if he was a messenger from God...

^   ^   ^

"I had an interesting thing happen at work," I said to Stephanie and the kids when I got home that evening. I told them all about my chance encounter and how encouraging it had been.

"Well, I have some news of my own," Stephanie said. "I talked with my family and they were asking questions about how to get tested."

That was the start of a flood of people who went to get tested on my behalf. One by one people went in to get checked, and it wasn't just Stephanie's side of the family.

When I went to church people would come up to me to tell me about the latest person who'd gone for testing.

"Did you hear who else went to get tested?" became a weekly question. I was always the last one to know. I thought it was kind of funny but because of the rules, I had no idea. I just stood there clueless, shocked, and humbled.

"Greater love has no one than this, that he lay down his life for his friends."

-John 15:13

I felt blessed to the point of tears. It would be like that every time I heard of how someone was getting tested for me— the thought of someone wanting to sacrifice their life for me. That is how I looked at it. This incredible, courageous act of sacrificial generosity was the most humbling feeling I had ever felt. These moments would lift me up to new levels of joy. They always came on those most trying days when I wondered, "How will I ever make it through?"

This was becoming even more important as things with dialysis were going worse. It was now the beginning of June. I was in my second month of dialysis and an odd thing was happening with each treatment. While most people have a dip in their blood pressure after dialysis, mine was going up. I had been in the Emergency room three different times after dialysis for high blood pressure and migraine headaches.

Hearing people were willing to donate for me was the blessing from God that helped me to continue on in the dark valley. To push on even when the pain and the fatigue were starting to take its toll; God was still in control. Hope was growing stronger. I took great comfort in knowing there were many people and churches throughout the community praying and caring for my family.

^   ^   ^   ^

By the middle of June, the rumors about people getting tested were coming pretty frequently. We tried to find out information but no one ever seemed to know much.

Then, one afternoon, TUMC called the house and talked to Stephanie, "Please stop sending donors." The person said, "We rarely see this many people come in to get tested for a single patient."

That shocked Stephanie. Again, we had no idea who or how many were going, we only heard rumors at church. The person from TUMC continued, "We have plenty. Unless they are a blood relative, please don't send anyone else."

We laughed because we hadn't really sent anyone to begin with. We didn't even know for sure who went up and got tested, just that there were quite a few.

Then they contacted us with the news we had been praying for.

"We have the guy we want to use."

^   ^   ^

It was a 25 year old young man named Eric Suter. He went to my church and had gone to get tested when his mom went; both were tested and Eric was a match.

I was ecstatic about Eric's kidney. He is a young guy, tall, strong, healthy. I'm thinking, "This is going to be a big kidney. It ought to run forever."

I wasn't the only person who was excited about this. Eric was pretty pumped to be able to help me.

I would joke around telling people "Eric and I had been in the Easter drama together at church since he was a teenager. I guess the thought of being chosen to give your kidney to "Jesus" must have seemed pretty cool."

Eric began his testing almost immediately.

Eric was buzzing right through all of the testing. He would push the nurses and doctor to keep moving him along at a fast pace. He was hurrying this process along like a man on a mission.

Finally, when his testing was complete, a date was set for the transplant!

July 15th.

Eric and his Grandmas

14

Hanging in There

When July came along, we were beginning to get excited. We were roughly two weeks away from surgery and it couldn't arrive soon enough. The dialysis was causing all kinds of problems each time I went. Furthermore, the two hour trips, twice a week were now three and a half hour appointments, three times a week.

The longer dialysis treatments were also followed by trips to the emergency room because my blood pressure was going higher and higher after each treatment. It was topping out at 210/115 and it was accompanied by massive migraine headaches and vomiting. No one could figure out why it was happening.

As much as I'd tried to keep some shred of normalcy, the kidneys won a few battles. One time, things were so bad that I'd been in the Intensive Care Unit (ICU).

That was painful for me physically and emotionally. It stole my chance to celebrate my daughter's graduation and everything.

Add to that all that my wife was going through. Stephanie had to coordinate everything on her own and I missed the whole doggone thing because of being sick. When I did end up getting home, it was Saturday night at about 9:00, after everybody was gone. She was just cleaning up from the whirlwind of people. Even as tired as she was, she cared for my needs

You'll understand that when you go through extreme moments like this, it's worse for the people looking in.

When I was going through it, I was in the eye of the hurricane. It was almost peaceful. Everything around me was completely chaotic. There were tests and trips, emotional highs and lows, but in the middle it was both agonizing and peaceful.

My sole focus was on getting well. Stephanie shouldered the burden of what I couldn't do. If you are, or have been a caregiver to someone going through a major illness or disease, your support means more to them than they can ever express to you.

I was experiencing emotions I couldn't understand or explain to Stephanie. I wanted to be the protector, caregiver, and father that I had been. Physically it was impossible to be all those things. Stephanie didn't make me feel bad about that. She was a source of strength and support to me.

Really, she demonstrated love in action. I know there were days when it was all too much for her. She broke down and cried more than once. She had her bad moments, but always—ALWAYS—I knew if I needed her, she was there.

Going through this was a hard and humbling experience. I'm a goal oriented person. I am completely driven.

When I'm focused, that is all there is. It makes her crazy how obsessive I am during these times in our marriage. I latch on to something and won't let go.

In 2010 my thing was staying alive.

There was nothing else going on. Everything else was to the side. Even my job was just there to keep making some money so we could keep the house.

She let me have that focus I needed. She didn't make me feel bad for what I couldn't do. She didn't badger me. She didn't focus on what she missed out on.

She supported me.

And when it was all over, and I knew I needed to do something special, she still supported me. She was ferociously protective. When she felt someone was doing wrong by me, she'd advocate for me.

I've always liked having company. During the illness when I had company, I felt better. It energized me and encouraged me. During those times Stephanie didn't complain. She helped host the group and clean up afterwards.

While everything going on around us was scary, Stephanie made the eye of the storm a calmer place.

I thank God that she was there for me.

I needed to have the surgery so I could go back to having a life. This was no way to live. It felt like an eternity since I'd felt well. Everything was a haze and I was weak and tired.

People have asked what it feels like when your kidneys are failing. The best answer that I've come up with is this example:

Picture yourself working a very hard 12 hour shift at work. Now, take that feeling and start your day out already feeling that exhausted. Add some symptoms that remind you of the flu. Things like aches and pains, a little nausea and headaches. Then your feet swell so bad you can't fit into your shoes any more. Your body moves in slow motion and you feel you're walking in a haze. You have to totally concentrate to stay focused. Physically, it isn't pleasant.

Renal failure doesn't stop there, however, because you have to monitor everything you eat. The diet doesn't allow any foods with phosphorous, potassium, or sodium.

I was taking over 27 pills each day. I had three different blood pressure pills, morning, noon and night with an extra fourth one in the evening. Despite that, my new normal blood pressure was 150 /100.

With all the drugs and toxins building in my body, my stomach felt ill most of the time. Despite my earlier appearance of health, my body was now showing the strain of the illness attacking it. I continued to work during this whole time. I held on to the hope of a day after the surgery when I'd feel good again.

That doesn't mean it was easy. On the days that I got too weak or felt dizzy, Stephanie drove me to work. At one point, it got so bad that I looked in to filing for temporary disability, but it paid only $190 per week before taxes and we knew we couldn't survive on that. Furthermore, we'd have to wait five months for the first check to arrive. Hopefully, by then this would all be over.

Apparently, paying in your whole life to the system does NOT have its benefits. They want you to be bankrupt before you can get it.

I held on, knowing this would all be over soon. The surgery would be here in just a couple of weeks. I only had to hold on until then.

While I tried not to think about it too much, I was starting to worry that I wasn't going to get a kidney in time. Dialysis, rather than saving me, seemed to make me worse. I was increasingly sick and tired. I didn't have any choice but to put the responsibility for everything in our house and life into Stephanie's hands. I was no kind of Dad to my daughters. I only existed from one dialysis appointment to the next.

From June in to July, my life was a matter of putting one foot in front of the other and living each day for the moment I could lay down again. Watching the days pass until I'd hopefully have my surgery.

I spent Independence Day stuck in bed suffering from another migraine. My blood pressure was through the roof again and Stephanie stayed by my side to care for me once again. It seemed the entirety of 2010 was falling into a chasm of my illness.

The normalcy of the life we'd had before no longer existed, and instead, we were living from one treatment to the next, one crisis to the next.

That doesn't mean we didn't still have good times, we did. Like so many others battling illness, we stole moments of joy in the midst of the struggle. You have to find joy, a way to still be happy, when you go through this or there is no way to survive emotionally.

The days following were filled with dialysis treatments and another ER visit. I'd given the situation over to God and trusted Him to bring me through—most days. The thing that kept me going was that the end was in sight.

An Angel named Willis...

I was in dialysis one day and things were not going well at all. My blood pressure was blowing over 200 consistently at this point during dialysis. The doctors were trying to get it figured out [which they never did], so I went each time knowing it was very possible that the night would end in the Emergency Room.

I was sitting in my chair in the dialysis room with a ring of people all in their chairs staring at the television or reading, anything to pass the time.

A few seats over was this little old man. His name was Willis. When Stephanie was there with me she sometimes went over and chatted with him a little bit. He was a very sweet, friendly fella, around 80 years old. He had a lifetime of experiences crowned by a full head of silver hair.

He always kept a little bag with him. He would finish, pick up this little bag, and walk out. He waddled with his hands out as if he was someone from the Wild, Wild West with a pair of six shooters. It always put a smile on my face.

One day, Stephanie was over talking to him for a little bit. He was finishing before me that day, so when he was nearly done, she came back over and sat with me. Dialysis lasts for three and a half hours, so he'd sometimes come and talk to me, too.

On this particular day, he came over and stuck his hand out to me.

"Hey, Willis, how you doing?" I reached through all the tubes and monitors to shake his hand.

He grabbed my hand tight and started praying like he was ticked off. There were twelve other people in the room, but Willis was not distracted by them.

He just started praying:

"Dear Heavenly Father, I pray in the name of Jesus that you would get this guy's blood pressure figured out. I pray that you bring his blood pressure down."

He was intense. He started getting louder. The prayer continued. The intensity of his prayers was like he was battling someone in the room.

"Amen," he said. Then he released my hand.

I looked up at him, "Thank you."

He just turned and walked away, didn't say a word.

That was really cool, but kind of weird at the same time. He didn't say a word. He didn't say a word when he walked up and he didn't say a word when he left. He just did it and walked away.

"Therefore, as we have opportunity, let us do good to all people, especially to those who belong to the family of believers."

-Galatians 6:10

I hate to admit it now, but I was a little bit uncomfortable at that time. I glanced around the room and the looks of the people were very matter of fact. A couple of the nurses were smiling at me, though.

One of the nurses I got to know, Heather, came over with a big grin on her face.

"That was pretty cool," I said.

"I thought it was, too," she replied.

I was going to present Willis with this book at the dialysis unit on the day of the release. But unfortunately, my friend Willis didn't make it. He went home to be with the Lord on August 1st 2011.

15

Abraham or Eric

By Monday, July 12th, I was deep into the valley of the shadow of death. I knew my time was running out and it was only a matter of time before something gave out. I also knew we were only days away from putting this entire thing behind us. We were about to overcome and conquer it all.

That day I had stayed home from work. Eric and his mom, Wendy, were going up to TUMC so he could have some last minute blood work for the surgery on Thursday.

At around 3:00 that afternoon, Wendy called.

"What does that mean?" Stephanie said. Her eyes were wide with shock and she moved back and forth. Something wasn't right. She glanced at me quickly, then away again.

"But?" Her voice vibrated with a mix between anger and, what was it? Confusion?

"Why not?" a pause, "How didn't they catch it?" Another pause. My stomach was starting to churn but this time it wasn't from the health problems. By Stephanie's reaction, I knew there was something awful going on. I felt helpless again. I didn't have the energy any longer to fight or to debate.

"Now what?" Tears were now running down her cheeks. I tried to get her attention, but she'd only give me the occasional glance and then looked away.

It was obvious I was losing the kidney. I felt almost numb from disappointment. The strength required to fight and keep me alive didn't leave much to fight this level of disappointment. All I could do was stare straight ahead in disbelief.

This couldn't be happening again. "God, where are you going with this?" We were so close.

Amy called Stephanie later and explained the situation. The surgery had been approved through the board and was on the schedule. Doctor Rees did not realize Eric had had the EBV virus (Mononucleosis) at one time.

"Doc said there is a chance that Troy could get Lymphoma cancer by this exchange," Amy had told Stephanie. "So he wouldn't put Eric's kidney in Troy with that risk."

"But we don't know that for sure," Stephanie said.

"I know, I tried to fight it," Amy had continued. "We have always done it this way in the past and it has never been a problem before."

"Well,.."

"So he challenged me to dig through all of his surgeries performed and see how many EBV infected kidneys were put into non-EBV recipients and what the outcomes were."

She finished the call by telling Stephanie she was going to continue to fight for us.

We were then scheduled for an appointment with Doctor Rees on Friday—the day AFTER I was supposed to have my new kidney—to go over the results and discuss our options.

As we struggled to make sense of it all, I continued to question God and his plan. "Everything happens for a reason," Stephanie kept saying.

To be honest I was sick of hearing it.

That was not what I wanted to hear at the moment, I was sick and tired of this roller coaster ride and just about had had enough. I was so miserable. Every day was a struggle without the constant disappointment. Why would He bring me so close and then pull the rug out yet again? And especially in the condition I was in now. Where was He going with all of this? Had He deserted me? Was I being punished?

"What strength do I have, that I should still hope? What prospects, that I should be patient? -Job 6:11

Though I was in shock, this time it felt different. I had someone else that had been through all of the testing and was standing right there with me.

Eric was extremely disappointed that he wasn't going to be able to help. He had prepared himself emotionally for what was coming. He'd gotten ready for his recovery period at home.

He'd told people what was coming up. He was probably even a little nervous.

When you think about it, I am sure he felt like the prize fighter that was days away from the title match and then was told "There's no fight."

He was sharing in my disappointment and I was upset for him. All the time, effort, emotion and stress he went through just to follow through with his decision. Then, to be told at the last second, "Oh, sorry, we can't use you."

I felt terrible for him and his family. They had all been so excited for us both, even Grandpa and Grandma Suter were rooting us on.

Stephanie and I continued to hold hope that Amy might be able to talk Doc into reconsidering. The fact was, this had never been an issue in the past. While Amy researched the files in the office, Stephanie got on the internet and began to search and see what the big deal was with this EBV situation.

She looked at information from the Mayo Clinic and Johns Hopkins to see what happened when EBV kidneys were placed in non-EBV recipients.

We quickly saw the issues.

98% of the public have had mononucleosis [EBV] at one time. Therefore, they have never worried too much about checking since it is so rare that a recipient would not have had it. That seemed to be pretty much the way it had always been done. However, there are more transplants now, so there is a sufficient sample to study.

What they had found was when they put the EBV kidney into a person who has never had it, 75% of the people get the mononucleosis virus. 75% of those people get Lymphoma Cancer and 25% of the people with cancer, die. Even more chilling was the fact that all of this happens within the first six months to a year after the transplant.

I looked at the statistics and an icy fear ran through my blood. I had always been the exception. If there was an 80/20, I was the 20. The whole way through this I'd beat the odds—for good and for bad.

I looked at Stephanie. "I'm going to die, I will be that 25%," She just looked at me. She understood.

Back when Dr Rees told me I was one of the healthiest patients he had ever seen, I didn't know it would end up being a curse. That was one of the reasons my brothers couldn't be used, because of the other virus they checked for (CMV). I didn't have that one either. The fact that I'd never had CMV only put me in a 45% group, but that was close enough to 50/50. I knew there was still a kidney out there for me. This was a 98% to 2% group. What were my odds now?

There was no reason to fight to get Eric's kidney. That would be my death sentence. All there was left to do at that point was to wait and talk to Dr. Rees on Friday, hoping for some options.

∧∧∧∧∧∧∧∧∧∧∧∧∧∧∧∧∧∧∧∧∧∧∧∧∧∧∧∧∧∧∧∧∧∧∧

"Then he reached out his hand and took the knife to slay his son. But the angel of the Lord called out to him from heaven, Abraham! Abraham!

"Here I am" he replied

"Do not lay a hand on the boy" he said. "Do not do anything to him. Now I know that you fear God, because you have not withheld from me your son, your only son."

Abraham looked up and there in a thicket he saw a ram caught by its horns. He went over and took the ram and sacrificed it as a burnt offering instead of his son. So Abraham called that place THE LORD WILL PROVIDE."

Genesis 22:10-14

The story of Abraham and Isaac reminds me of Eric and his kidney. As Abraham made his way up the mountain to sacrifice his son, Eric was climbing his own mountain of sorts. Just as he had completed all of his preparations and was ready to go through with it, God would say "You have proven yourself. You were willing, but I am going to provide for myself another."

Though I did not know that at the time...

16

300

So as Friday came, here we are in mourning again. What are we going to do? We're on pins and needles constantly, up and down the roller coaster. It seems like things are getting better and they are almost ready to bust out and then CRASH they go back down again—except there is no exhilaration when you fly down. It is more a sense of terror-laden freefall as you try to grab around you for some stability.

This was one more barrier we needed to find a way around.

On Friday we were still up in the air on what to do. We knew the possibilities of taking Eric's kidney and what it could do to me. But we also knew time was limited for me either way. We just needed some direction.

So, as we entered the exam room and sat down to wait on Amy and Dr. Rees, I noticed the computer monitor. I tapped Stephanie on the leg and said, "Look". Flashing on the screensaver were the words, "We have always done it this way." with a big red circle around it and a line slashed through it.

Talk about a billboard. Those were the words Amy had been saying all week. I looked at Stephanie and said "We're not using Eric." I guess the Lord was computer savvy.

When Dr. Rees and Amy walked in, Doc began explaining the situation. He started out by telling us why taking Eric's kidney was a problem. He reiterated the fact that there was a very high possibility that I would get the EBV virus (mononucleosis) and then Lymphoma cancer.

I knew that from Stephanie's research, but I wanted to see what Amy's investigation had turned up. Obviously, I was hoping for some positive news.

Doc went through the results; out of the more than 300 surgeries there were only four cases where an EBV virus kidney was put into a recipient that had never had it before. Three out of the four had contracted mononucleosis and all three ended up with Lymphoma cancer. One died.

"We primarily check for two viruses that are in a person's system. These are things that they would have caught earlier in life and are no longer a problem for them." Doc said. "It would, however, be a problem if it was put into a person that had never had the disease before."

I listened. I knew this from our research. I appreciated him explaining all of it, but I was waiting for the "but", the exception that would make it possible for me to have surgery. Instead, it got worse.

"Since you never had either one of these viruses, you are in a very rare situation. 45% and 2% of each bracket along with the fact that you are A positive." His face was kind, his eyes intelligent. "That gives you roughly a 1 in 400 chance of finding a match. That doesn't even take into account the antigen scale that goes from 1-6 with 6 being a perfect match."

I listened as he continued with facts, like how long I'd have to wait [twice as long] and what that could mean [possibly 5 years], as well as who my likely donor would be [a 15 yr old boy who died suddenly without ever having had either virus].

I sat there in complete shock. I wanted to formulate questions, offer some meaningful suggestion or rebuttal, but the weight of disappointment was too intense.

"You've gotta be kidding me?" was all I could eek out. I felt helpless. I turned and looked at Stephanie.

Suddenly, Stephanie looked at the Doc and got very serious. Her protective instincts took over like that of a mother protecting her young. Her eyes held the intensity of a woman on a mission. We trusted Doc, and she needed to know if this was the absolute answer.

She looked straight at him and said, "Look, mano to mano, man to man," and that's exactly how she said it, "Forget you're a doctor. Knowing everything he's been through, if you were him, what would you do?"

The room got very quiet. I was thinking to myself, "Whoa! That lady has some guts."

Later, Amy told us she'd been working with Doc for a long time and she'd never heard anyone go toe to toe with him like that. It wasn't a moment of disrespect or questioning his education. It was the exact opposite. Stephanie needed to know in that moment what a man who is an expert in this would do if it was his own life on the line.

We both needed to know that we would make the absolute right choice. This was a life and death decision. There was no guarantee that another kidney was available. There was no indication that we could get one in time, even.

Doc deals with life and death every day. He deals with the reality that the decisions he makes and the information he shares will impact a person—for better or for worse—for the rest of their lives.

He sat down in his chair and he leaned back. His eyes were focused on me as if studying me. Then he sighed and stared again.

Even now I'm impressed with the seriousness with which he considered Stephanie's question. He wasn't giving a canned answer or something out of a "How to Relate to your Patient Effectively" handbook. He was putting himself in my place. He was considering all he knew about my symptoms, my lab results, my chances of survival...all of it.

He was considering me as a person. He was wondering what he would do in that situation. He was really listening.

It felt like an eternity. Him watching me. Thinking. Shifting. Thinking more.

"Well…" he broke the silence with a single word that didn't hold the confidence of a physician, but instead, the uncertainty of a man.

"Well," he began again. "Knowing everything he's gone through and how the dialysis is not working…" he looked between Stephanie and me again. Then he formed his words very carefully.

"If it were me, I'd probably go with Eric."

Remarkably, that's not what I wanted to hear. Essentially, he was saying he truly believed, knowing EVERYTHING he did about my condition and my circumstances, he would feel more comfortable with the risk of death than with my chances on dialysis and waiting for a donor.

"Wow," was all I could say.

What else can you say? I was dumbfounded.

He continued, "Look. If you check yourself," he moves his hands from his neck to his arm pits and down his body to simulate checking his lymph nodes for swelling. "If you're just fanatic about it," he looked me directly in the eye, "I'll make sure you don't die."

I was completely floored. I stared at him for a long moment, then looked at Steph and glanced at Amy. Their faces mirrored my emotions. Their eyes said, "I can't believe you just said that. You can't guarantee somebody that."

At that moment Doc became ten feet tall and bullet-proof to me. From that point forward, what he says goes.

"What else can we do, Doc?" Steph asked.

"Well," he said, "There is another option. We have started a program here called Alliance for Paired Donation. (APD)"

Here's how it works. If you have a loved one that wants to give you their kidney, but is unable to for whatever reason, they can be matched up with a stranger that needs a kidney within the APD network across the nation. You would in turn receive a kidney from someone else's loved one.

This would, in essence, be like giving you a kidney where you wouldn't otherwise have received one.

So, someone gives a kidney to me, my friend/loved one gives a kidney to someone else then the chain continues. By paying it forward, it is a living chain. This will allow you to be matched up with a donor to allow for a transplant much sooner.

At the time, Doc was explaining that there were about 300 kidneys across the country of live donors in the network. Those are all people ready and willing to donate.

"Maybe we'll find one," he said

I thought to myself. Wow, I am holding all of my hopes on "Maybe we'll find one" when I knew my odds were 1 in 400.

He continued, "That doesn't include the antigen scale. That sets it off into a whole 'nother bracket."

He said, "But here's the deal, we need an O blood donor."

All of us turned to look at Amy. She stood against the wall, with a look of concern on her face. She shook her head from side to side.

"They're all A?!" Doc exclaimed. "You've *got* to be kidding me," he said, just as I had so many times before.

We were all thinking the same thing. Not a single O? Out of a dozen people? I had told everybody I'd take an O or an A. I thought for sure somebody would be an O.

We all sat in silence for a moment, as Doc calculated the next move.

"Wait a minute. Isn't one of my brothers an O?" I asked, hope again rising. "I'm pretty sure one of my brothers is an O." Amy started to say no.

"Go get the files," Doc said.

She went out the door. I watched for her to come back. When she did, she was looking through the chart, walking in slow motion.

"Tony's an O," she said slowly as in disbelief. Stephanie and I just looked at each other smiling. We knew there was a glimmer of hope and that was all we needed at this point.

"Do you think he'll do it?" Doc asked.

"I'm pretty sure he'll do it," Of course in my head I thought "He better do it".

Doc said, "My wife heads up the APD network. We are going to spend the weekend putting your numbers into the system. We will scour the country and see if we can find at least one match. We will call you Sunday with the results."

Hopefully out of 300 we will find the one.

^^

As the news was getting worse, so were the odds. Sometimes it seems like God has to take us to impossible lows, stack the odds completely against any natural way out, so that faith and the hope in things not yet seen is all you have left. He wants to be sure no man can take credit and all glory is given where it is deserved.

When you reach this point, the credit can only be given to the one that did the supernatural. Just as in the story of Gideon and the 300. He started with 32,000 men and ended up with 300 to face the tens of thousands of Midianites.

"The Lord said to Gideon, "You have too many men for me to deliver Midian into their hands. In order that Israel may not boast against me that her own strength has saved her,"
-Judges 7:2

"The Lord said to Gideon, "With the 300 men that lapped I will save you and give the Midianites into your hands. Let all the other men go, each to his own place."
-   Judges 7:7

17

Songs of Hope

We spent the entire weekend trying for a sense of normalcy, but our full attention was on Sunday afternoon. What would we find out? Would there be a donor? While I'd always been the exception, the odds were not in my favor on this one.

When Dr. Rees called Sunday afternoon, Stephanie answered. I was sitting on the couch resting, battling nerves and fatigue.

"Oh my gosh! That is wonderful news Doctor."

Her words, and the excitement in her voice, stirred me out of my lethargy.

She looked at me and put up two fingers. I rushed over and sat down next to Stephanie. "Put him on speaker so I can hear."

Doc continued, "One donor is in Pennsylvania and the other is in Colorado. The guy in Pennsylvania is willing to come here and lay side-by-side with you and do the surgery but the guy in Colorado is not."

No brainer—I knew the guy in Pennsylvania was my ideal donor. Close and the kidney would barely be out of the body before it was in me.

"Two people." I said, feeling positively exceptional.

"Yes," Doc said. "And I want to go with the guy in Colorado."

What? Again, it seemed that what I saw as the right thing was being challenged. I started the math. It doesn't take a genius to realize the kidney would be out of the body a very long time.

I trusted Doc, but what he was saying to me didn't make much sense at all. "Would that be like a cadaver kidney, Doc? I'll only get half the time as a live kidney."

"No," he said without hesitation. "I'm not going to lie. It's going to be out of the body for a long time. It'll be one of the longest ones we've ever done, but it's a live kidney."

"Okay."

I still wasn't entirely convinced. I trusted Doc, really I did, but it just seemed like the more likely pick was Pennsylvania kidney, not other-side-of-the-country kidney.

To his credit, Doc was willing to be patient and address my concerns.

"Troy, here's the deal. If you go with the guy from Pennsylvania, you're going to be fifth in line. These things have a way of falling through by the time they get to you. The guy from Colorado is an altruistic donor. That means he showed up to the clinic one day and wanted to give his kidney away to a stranger. He doesn't care who he's giving it to. This means he has no bindings to anybody"

"Okay."

Then Doc said what I'd been praying to hear, "And, you'll be first in line."

YES!

"The chain can't be broken," Doc said. "It's possible that we could get this done in the next couple of weeks if everything works out."

"Oh my gosh, that is awesome Doc!" I exclaimed.

He laughed, "Well, it's not done yet. We still have some things to work out. The guy from Colorado has some issues he needs to deal with before we finalize surgery, but we'll know more about that on Monday. In the meantime, talk to your brother Tony and make sure he is ready to go. He will have a lot of testing to do in a very short period of time. We will want to start right away."

We hung up the phone and we sat there in surreal disbelief. We were smiling. Hope was building.

"I can't believe it. Not one, but two donors out of 300," I said.

Even though we were excited, we knew we still had to call Tony and blindside him with this question.

It had been two months since he was rejected and the last he'd heard Eric was a match. So going through this surgery was nowhere on his radar. Then, there is the fact that people get funny when they find out their kidney is not going directly to you, but to a stranger. Add to that, he was the only O donor of everyone tested.

That made this call very crucial. All of my hopes and dreams of a 2nd chance at life were riding on my big brother. He was all I had and I was all in. So needless to say, I was a little nervous to call him.

Before I could make the call, Stephanie and I went out for a drive. The sun was shining on this beautiful July day. It made me feel better and further built up my hope. We prayed, and then I dialed the cell phone.

When he answered, I started in with small talk to ease in to the big questions. I explained about Eric and the viruses. Then I moved on to the APD program and told him how that worked.

"They have found a donor for me. But in order to receive it, I have to have a loved one that is an O donor. You are my..."

"No problem, little brother."

No hesitation. No questions. Just agreement. I lost it. I broke down crying. The emotion of the moment overwhelmed me and I let it all flood out. All of the fear, confusion, pain, anguish, and even hope, gushed out in a torrent of tears.

I sat there unable to talk from emotion.

"Are you there? Are you there?! Troy, I said I would do it," Tony said.

"Yeah," it was all I could get out. I started bawling again. Deep wracking sobs. This was really going to be over. This time all the bases were covered. We had a match. He would do it. Tony would do it.

I had a kidney. I was going to live.

Not only live, but thrive. For nearly a year, I'd done little more than exist between hospital visits and treatments. I'd gone through an entire year dragging myself to work and back, hoping that soon it would be over. All the while, things kept getting worse.

But now it was almost over. I couldn't hold it back any more.

Tony's voice was soothing on the other end of the phone, "It's alright, buddy. It's okay." He was talking to me like I was a little kid. "It's okay. Hey, man," he continued, "I said yes."

Steph and I were in the car watching the scenery fly by. I couldn't hand the phone to Stephanie because she was bawling, too, at this point. She had to pull over.

Finally, I try to hold my breath and gain my composure. "Thank you," I said. "You have no idea…"

"It's not a problem. What do I gotta do?"

That question helped me to focus again. There was a surgery to plan. "I'm not sure at this point. Doc's going to contact you and you'll have to do a whole bunch of testing."

"Okay, not a problem. That's not a problem."

"Okay," I said. We talked about it for just a little bit longer before we got off the phone. Afterwards, I felt a little foolish for breaking down the way I did. Stephanie and I laughed about it later, thinking Tony must have thought I lost my mind.

I hadn't lost anything though. I'd regained my life.

^   ^   ^

"Speak to one another with psalms, hymns and spiritual songs. Sing and make music in your heart to the Lord,"

- Ephesians 5:19

During these times, I listened to the radio for inspiration. I heard different songs during these weeks that would inspire me. It was almost as if God himself was speaking to me, singing to me. He was letting me know He was with me and we only had a little farther to go.

I bet you probably do the same thing—if not I would highly recommend it. It's really an encouraging way to get through your trials in life.

We pulled out and began to drive home after talking with Tony. I turned on the radio and a song was playing on a station called K-LOVE. The song had kind of been our theme song during this whole thing. It was by a newer Christian singer named Josh Wilson and the song was "Before the Morning".

18

Raging Hope

On Monday, we received the call that our donor from Colorado would be able to get off work for the surgery and recovery. Evidently, that must have been the possible snag that Doc was waiting on. The donor had started a brand new job and had to see if it was alright to get the time off. Keep in mind that he is a complete stranger and I did not find out this information until well after the surgery took place.

I got the call telling me someone needed my kidney at a somewhat inopportune time.

I had gone in months ago saying I wanted to donate my kidney if someone needed it. I figured it would happen pretty quickly, but after a couple of months I almost felt like they'd forgotten me.

When I got the call that weekend, the person I talked to explained there was a program, Alliance For Paired Donation, where you participate as an altruistic donor to start a transplant chain.

The person said, "And we had a chain set up, but the donor, at the last minute, fell through and wasn't a match. And you are actually a match. Would you be willing? Oh by the way, this would be a week and a half from today."

I was so excited and so bummed all at once. I realized there was no way I could do it. I just got hired on this new job. It was a corporate job. **Monday was going to be my first day.**

"I have committed to be in training for the next eight weeks without any absences," I said. I really felt like there would be no way to do it, but I agreed to ask the next day when I went for my first week of training.

I prayed. I wasn't sure what I could do or if it would work out.

And a miracle happens. I went to work in the morning and sat through the first morning session. We learned one of the pillars of the company was,

"Do the right thing, because it's the right thing to do."

I tucked that away because I was about to live it.

When we broke for lunch, I grabbed the HR contact in the room and asked if I could speak with her privately for a moment.

I just laid it all out. "Here's the deal," I said. "I have this opportunity to donate my kidney to someone who needs it. I don't want to miss this opportunity."

I didn't give her a chance to respond, I just kept going, "All these pieces fell into place because it's supposed to happen. You taught us this morning to 'do the right thing because it is the right thing to do', but I need your permission, your understanding, to know that I could miss anywhere from two weeks to six weeks of time in order to do this."

I looked at her and said, "What would you do?"

"Let me see what my superiors say." I continued with training and around two that afternoon she pulled me aside.

"They are fine with it and they think it's fantastic. They're very impressed with your tie-ins with the core values of the company."

It was great, the support I got. They actually sent an email out to management about me.

Λ   Λ   Λ   Λ

Things started moving along again. The following day, Tuesday July 21st, Tony began his testing process. For each test, he drove two and a half hours—one way—down from Michigan to Toledo, OH to perform various tests, then two and a half hours home after they were done.

Michigan had been in a recession for a few years by that time. It hit a number of people hard, and my brother was no exception. Tony had been out of work for a while. He was a welder by trade and an ordained minister as well. He still served as a preacher on different Sundays since he did not have a church of his own, but he didn't have regular work.

Tony's 53 years old, never goes to the doctor and has no health insurance. That meant he hadn't had a check up in a long time. Since he was donating, all of the tests were covered by the recipient's insurance. He would not have to pay a dime for the tests!

When they start running him through these tests, the first thing they did was a series of x-rays, including a chest x-ray, just to see how his heart and lungs were doing.

"Well, you've had a heart attack at one time," one of the doctors said to him.

"I've never had a heart attack." Tony lifts weights and exercises all the time. He's a pretty healthy guy and figured he'd remember a heart attack.

"What we're seeing here says you have, so we're going to send you down to the heart unit."

He went down to the heart unit. He was greeted by a woman in scrubs. "Okay. We're going to do a treadmill stress test on you today."

In retrospect, it was amazing how quickly things got done. He didn't have to set up appointments and drive back and forth to the hospital. He just walked down and they got him right in to the heart lab to do the treadmill stress test.

"We're still not satisfied. Can you come back tomorrow and we'll do a heart catheterization on you?"

"Are you serious?!?" I asked him when he told me what happened.

"Yeah. I have to go back tomorrow and do a heart catheterization."

So he drove the long trip home, and then back, the next day to perform this test.

When he went in the next day, they found only 10% blockage and ended up telling him he had never had a heart attack. A confirmation to what he already knew.

~ 157 ~

After the heart catheterization, they ran a few other tests and decided they saw something in his colon that needed to be checked. He was told to come back the following day to perform a Colonoscopy. If there was anything there, this could prevent him from being used.

Thursday, he had the Colonoscopy and was told everything was great. He was ready for more tests.

The tests continued the rest of the week until Friday, when I received a call from Tony.

"Well, little brother, I might be getting shot down."

"What? What now?" This wasn't happening. Not again. I was again days from getting a kidney and being told that again the kidney was not mine to have. How many times would this happen?

"Well," he said, "They found two cysts on my kidneys. They found one that's about the size of a fist on one and a small cyst on the other."

"They're not going to use them if they have cysts on them," I said.

After hanging up, I turned to Stephanie and said "Text the Army!" She knew exactly what that meant.

She had compiled three or four different groups that she could text at any one time. They were the prayer warriors. They ranged from individuals to churches, which then send out the prayer request to others by way of a chain.

A few hours later, we got a call, "We're still good. They'll be able to use them."

That was great news for me, but I assumed I was going to now be leaving my brother with only one kidney, and that one had a cyst on it the size of a fist.

When I said that, he said, "Actually, the recipient is going to get the kidney with the larger cyst. I am going to keep the kidney with the small cyst on it."

In Tony's case, it turned out that it's kind of a soft cyst they can work around and remove or drain. That kidney would go to a man in Florida and it would be safe for him to have.

We were good. We were going to continue on.

He had a full medical workup free of charge to him. It was all picked up by the recipient's insurance. These are medical tests he wouldn't have likely done because he was uninsured, but each test pointed to a potential problem.

That led to another test. And at the end of the week, Tony had a clean bill of health with the exception of the cysts. And it was all free of charge.

∧∧

My health was failing fast and there were the worries that I could have a stroke if my blood pressure didn't stop climbing. Despite this, the weaker my body became, the stronger my Hope in the future was growing.

It felt like the final stretch of a marathon and I was almost out of gas, I had almost nothing left. I'd hit the wall and was pushing through. I was crawling to the finish, but I could feel something rising up within me. A strength that I didn't know was there.

I was less than a week away from my 2nd chance at life and things were looking very promising. I could see the light at the end of the tunnel. This strength was building inside of me. Though I was weak and ill, something was changing...

It was The HOPE giving me a 2nd wind and it was carrying me at this point. It was all I had and it was inside of me raging!

"But those who hope in the Lord will renew their strength. They will soar on wings like eagles; they will run and not grow weary, they will walk and not be faint."

-Isaiah 40:31

19

Walking in the Valley

I had hoped dialysis was going to work better than it did. Everyone else in there seemed to do fine; it was just this rare thing that was happening to me.

While I'd once thought of dialysis as an inconvenience, it was now a life and death struggle. For whatever reason, my body seemed to fight every effort I took to save it. On the Friday Tony finished up his testing, I also had a dialysis treatment. My blood pressure at the end of dialysis had hit 235 over 125 and I ended up in the ER again.

The Following Monday

I woke up and sat at the edge of the bed for a moment, my head throbbing. The room was still dark and quiet. I put my head in my hands and fought to muster up the strength to start another day. The effort of simply sitting seemed to steal all of my energy. The room swirled around me. My elbows dug into my thighs from the weight of supporting my head.

"You can do this, I thought to myself. "We're almost done." I willed myself to stand. I kept encouraging my muscles and bones to muster enough strength to get up one more time.

I lifted myself up and slowly made my way to the bathroom and flipped on the light. The brightness strengthened the force of my headache and I squinted away from it. I opened the drawer full of pills and, one by one, pulled out the 27 different pills that kept me alive. This was my morning routine.

Suddenly, it was as if an explosion was erupting in my skull. I dropped to my knees and threw my face over the toilet. My stomach squeezed tighter and tighter and I dry heaved until yellow bile came. This was becoming a step in my morning routine.

Tears of pain and despair welled up. I leaned away from the toilet. "How much longer will I have to endure this agony? Dear Heavenly Father, please allow this to end soon," I begged.

I slowly got control of my emotions again, stood up, and cleaned myself off. Then I started to take my pills. I brushed my teeth and attempted to get dressed.

Next, I opened the cupboard and grabbed the blood pressure cuff, then made my way to the kitchen. I pulled the chair out at the kitchen table and sat down, wrapped the blood pressure cuff around my right arm, and began pumping it up.

I sat there with my head resting in my hand and my eyes closed waiting for the reading. The digital display read 184 over 117. Would I be able to drive the 50 minutes one way to work and open the doors for one of the employees who needed to get in early today?

Stephanie walked in the room. "How bad is it?"

"Not good," I murmured. "184/117 and I haven't even done dialysis yet."

"You're not going to work. I am taking you to the emergency room!" Her voice was far sterner than I'd expected. She reminded me that I had about 3% of my kidneys left. "It's time to stop trying to be a hero."

"Okay," I whispered. I was in no mood to argue.

So at 5:45am on Monday, July 26th, my wife drove me to the hospital ER.

"Good morning Troy and Stephanie," the nurse said with a kind smile. "Troy, go on back so they can hook you up. Stephanie, I'll get some papers around for you to fill out."

A nurse came in and began to hook me up to the machine that checks your vitals continuously. She turned it on.

"Your blood pressure is really high," she said. "Have you had a headache or any vomiting?" Before I could answer, I started vomiting. Stephanie was just walking in the room and, again, she had to see me at my worse.

By the time I finished vomiting, the nurse had all the answers she needed. She put an IV in me and walked out to get the doctor.

After about ten minutes, the doctor came in and began asking a series of his own questions. He prescribed the same medication that took the pain away and brought the blood pressure down previous times. Then he walked out.

I lie in the bed and tried to remind myself that this was all almost over. Stephanie stood up and walked over to my side and put her hand on my forehead. She gently kissed me on the cheek.

"I love you," she said. Her glassy eyes were intense. She smiled, but was full of emotion.

I looked up at her and whispered, "I love you, too." She turned from me and sat down next to the bed. A single tear broke away and slid down my cheek.

I turned my head to look at her and we stared at each other until I shut my eyes. "God, where are you going with this ride?" I silently prayed. "And how much longer will I have to hang on?"

^   ^   ^

The medicine was doing its work and they released me from the ER. Around 11:00 am, we got home from the hospital and I went to bed to sleep off the medication. I hoped I'd feel a little better.

Somewhere around 2:00 in the afternoon I started to wake up. My mind was in the foggy blur that comes from deep sleep, only it didn't slide away to lucidity. I was in disarray and couldn't focus very well. It was as if I was dreaming but I was awake.

I was both cold and hot. Panic started to grab my mind and gave me enough clarity to recognize that there was a wet feeling all over me. It was as if someone poured a bucket of water over me while I was asleep. I pulled the covers away with what strength I could muster and looked around.

The bed was soaked from head board to footboard. I leaned on one arm to try to get up and saw sweat forming a river down my arm and dripping to the sheets. It was as if I was sitting in a 130 degree sauna.

I couldn't remember the last time I'd sweated.

A new sensation now grabbed hold. Panic followed by something odd. It was a cold, hollow, empty feeling. With no frame of reference that was the best way I can explain it. Tied to it was a sense of pain and panic. Was this what death felt like?

I sat up on the edge of the bed and I looked down. Sweat continued streaming down my arms. I felt weak. Maybe I really was dying. I didn't know. I'd had so many different ailments and feelings by this time. This was very different. This was a scary emptiness.

Something was very wrong.

My kidneys were shutting down and my body was going into defense mode. It had been pushed to the brink.

"Steph-a-nie," my voice was barely more than a strained whisper.

How she heard me I will never know, but she did. I heard her come down the hall. She was there in a flash.

"Oh my gosh, what's going on?" She charged into our bedroom door and looked me over.

"I don't know but something's not right," I strained, "Do something."

She ran for the phone and called the dialysis unit.

"They said to get you to Toledo Hospital NOW!" She came beside me quickly to help me get ready. "Are you going to make it?"

"I don't know," I answered and then I got up. I don't remember getting to the van.

She started driving down the road. The Fremont Hospital came in to view. We drive past that to get to the Toledo Hospital 45 minutes away.

I saw the hospital getting closer and considered the distance.

"I'm scared, pull in," I said.

She cranked the car in without a moment's hesitation. She took me right up to the Emergency Room doors and I climbed out.

"We need to get to Toledo Hospital," I managed to say.

I really don't remember much but soon I started vomiting non-stop. We waited for an ambulance to come get me. Then, they put me into an ambulance and hauled me up to Toledo Hospital.

Things blurred past. From one hospital to the next. From the dialysis unit to my own room. The next 14 hours I struggled to stay awake and alive. At 4:00 a.m., I was moved from the room I'd been in over to the ICU where I was put on nitroglycerine to control the blood pressure. It had been 22 straight hours of shuffling. I'm not sure how Stephanie stayed awake but, at 4 am when I was settled in the ICU, she left for the hour drive home.

At around 7:30am, my phone rang and woke me up. It was Stephanie.

"Hello," I started to say, but she trampled over my greeting.

"You're not going to believe this."

"What?"

"I just hung up with Amy. Your surgery's tomorrow."

I was stunned. "Oh my gosh! Did you tell her where I'm at?"

"Yeah, I did. She said she'd call me back and hung up on me."

I already knew they wouldn't do the surgery if I was in that condition. Did I come this far just to lose my kidney again? I leaned my head back, "Are you on your way?"

"I'm leaving right now."

Stephanie was running on two hours of sleep and, by that point, was surviving on pure adrenaline.

I closed my phone and set it beside me with a sigh. I put my head back and just closed my eyes in meditation. For the next few minutes, I thought about what had happened the day before, and how near I was to dying. I came to the realization that this was probably my last 2nd chance at life; and that if it didn't happen I was probably not going to last much longer.

"For if we live, we live to the Lord; and if we die, we die to the Lord. So, whether we live or die, we belong to the Lord's"

Romans 14:8

Then, suddenly a funny thing happened. There was a peace that came over me. It was like I was fine no matter what happened. I finally knew without a shadow of a doubt that God was in control and I was good with it.

He was going to either deliver me or take me home and that was okay with me. At that moment it became very surreal, as if everything was going to be okay. I no longer feared what I did not know, I only trusted in the One that knew.

"Even though I walk through the valley of the shadow of death,
I will fear no evil,
    for you are with me;
    your rod and your staff,
    they comfort me"
                    -Psalms 23:4

20

The Awakening

Tuesday

I was resting in the quietness of the room, basking in my newfound freedom from fear. Suddenly, two doctors burst in to my room followed by about four other people. I looked up quickly at all of them, and tried to take in everything that was happening.

One man looked at me, "Mr. Lewis we're going to take you to TUMC right now." They moved me to their cot and wheeled me out. Within 15-20 minutes I was in another ICU over at TUMC.

In the space of less than 5 minutes, Amy had called and handled everything. How was that possible? That always amazed me and still does to this day.

What was also amazing was the fact that Amy called that early in the morning. She had never called that early. Normally she'd made calls to us in the afternoon, but she was so excited to tell us the surgery was the next day, that she couldn't wait to call us.

So, the surgery was scheduled for Wednesday. When I got settled in the ICU at TUMC, I had two nurses tending to me nonstop throughout the day. In order for the surgery to go ahead, I had to get my blood pressure down and I had to be off of the nitroglycerine. If they didn't succeed, I wouldn't be able to have the surgery.

Visitors paraded in and out of my room throughout the day. They came with words of encouragement as well as prayer. My mother-in-law (Debbie), brought Allison and Corrine up to hang out with Stephanie and me. It was very comforting to have my family all together, supporting me. As I told you before, I like having people around.

As day gave way to night and night to morning, we waited for signs of improvement. My blood pressure wasn't staying down on its own without the nitro. It was now a sprint to get me off of it. The nurses came every half hour to an hour to try to notch me down a little lower. They were ever watchful of my BP.

Understand that they had taken the kidney in Colorado at 8:00 am and it was on the way here. If they didn't get me off of the nitro and fast, the kidney was going to the man from Florida who was supposed to get Tony's kidney.

In the midst of the friends, family, and nurses, Amy had been in and out all morning to check on me. We could sense the intensity and the urgency of this race. The revolving nurses continued. We all watched the numbers.

Normally you're not allowed many visitors, but the nurses were kind enough to allow me the people. All day long people were rolling in. There were people from church, family members, my daughters' friends, and friends of the family.

All of these people had helped us out through this whole thing so far. Now they all came to see the victory at the end. None of us expected any less.

Zeke and Jake were there. Tony and his wife Marcia came in. They were praying in my room. Then, they went in the hall to pray with other people. There was a lot of praying going on.

Then, a pastor came in and handed me a prayer blanket. I thought that was really cool.

"I want to get one of those," Tony said.

In an odd kind of way, it was an almost festive atmosphere. It made me feel good to have all of these people around me, happy, believing everything would now be okay. It almost helps you forget how miserable you feel and how dire the circumstances were at that moment.

It gave me hope.

The day went by pretty quickly. This was my one shot. I knew it. It was "do or die"—literally. It is funny that when we were waiting all those long months for a kidney to come, we kept wishing it would hurry up. Time felt like it was dragging through the hour glass.

Now that the kidney was on its way, I had hoped time would slow down so my body would be ready.

Before I realized it, Doc walked in. It was about two or three in the afternoon.

"How are you doing?" he asked.

I felt pretty miserable, but that had been the case for a while. Considering the circumstances, how should I feel?

I looked at him and tried to smile, "You tell me."

His eyes were smiling, "You're doing good." He put his hand on the rail of my bed, "We're going to go for it."

Yes!

Then it was just like BAM! As if someone flipped a switch, everyone was excited. The people who had been milling in and out of my room were cheering and celebrating.

Everyone started surging in my room. We were all excited. We'd endured to the end. This was all almost over. Tomorrow morning, for real this time, I'd wake up with a new kidney. I'd be whole again. I'd function like I had before this calamity hit.

But we still had to get the kidney here and there was one more battle to overcome.

It had been weeks since we had seen a severe thunderstorm. As God would have it, outside one of the worst summer storms we'd seen all season was raging. That was going to slow it down.

The kidney was on its way in. It had now spent a number of hours out of the donor's body, going from the hospital to the airport, from Denver to Detroit and then nearly two hours down the interstate to where I was.

We'd known it would be a long trip and that it would spend a long time out of the body, but the weather just wasn't cooperating with us at all.

Time slowed down for me again while we waited for the kidney to arrive.

"You want to see if we can go down early?" Doc asked me, his excitement matching mine.

"Sure."

"I'll go see what I can do."

Doc disappeared out of the room and I continued to push through the last of this discomfort. This was really going to happen. Unless you've experienced something like this you really cannot understand the level of anticipation—the thought of being whole again.

Those of you who have experienced this alongside me, you know what it is like to wait for that surgery. You want to get to the operating room and get things started. You want to know that nothing will go wrong. You won't be satisfied until you're awake with your new life.

There can be so much disappointment when waiting for an organ transplant. People who change their mind or who aren't a match compound the disappointment. I'd faced so much of it, but now the kidney was only a few miles from me and headed my way. My donor was likely awake in recovery, never fully realizing what his sacrifice would mean to me.

And we waited.

About a half hour later, Doc returned. His face was almost like that of a disappointed child, "They won't let us go down until the kidney shows up."

"Alright," I said.

He left the room and I occupied myself with idle chit-chat and watching the clock.

A little while later, Doc came in the room.

"It just showed up. Let's go."

They started wheeling me down the hallways, and everyone was following me. It is amazing that something so life changing can actually be more of a celebration than a dangerous surgery.

I was getting lots of hugs, kisses, and well-wishes. The anesthesiologist had already introduced himself to me during the pre-op consultation, so I recognized him.

"Are you ready?" he asked.

"Yes, I am. I am so ready."

"Alright, as soon as I hit this button you're going to feel good for a little bit and then we'll get going."

"Okay."

He pushed the button and I felt very weird and goofy.

"Go ahead and lay back."

"Alright."

I laid back and they started wheeling me into the surgery. The world was spinning. It was a bit surreal. I felt like I couldn't fully form a thought. The wheels clanked down the hall reminding me of when I fell asleep in the car as a child. I closed my eyes in a long blink and looked around.

Lights on the ceiling.

I blinked a second time. The lights were still there. I'm clicking through the hall. I hadn't realized it would take so long to get down there.

Then it hits me. I've had the surgery.

"Is it over?" I said reluctantly.

"Yes," The nurse replied with a surprised smile on her face.

Groggy confusion. Then fear. I didn't hurt. With the way my journey had progressed recently, thoughts started pounding in my mind.

Maybe they didn't go through with it. Maybe something happened? They got in there, they couldn't do it.

Thoughts bombarded my head.

I looked again at the nurse and wondered if I dared to ask the next question. I mustered up all the courage I could build. "How'd it go?"

"Honey, it went wonderful. It was one of the smoothest surgeries we've ever had."

The tears gushed. "Thank you, Jesus," I said through my sobs.

Relief washed over me.

Stephanie was next to me as we wheeled down the hall. She was laughing. Later she would explain it was because she thought that it was the drugs making me cry. At the moment, I was too caught up in the moment to worry about why she was laughing. I had my kidney. It had really happened.

"Thank you, Jesus!" I cried out a second time. I cried. Absolute joy and relief filled me with gratefulness. The feelings lingered for a few moments longer and then I passed out. Surgery was finished at 30 minutes past midnight. It was a new day for us, literally and figuratively. I was out, but Stephanie was wide awake and had time to think as I slept.

From talking to her, I really think at that moment she fully realized what all of this meant to us. How our life was changing again to a post-renal failure life.

She had spent so many long months loving me, caring for me, shuttling me to doctor appointments and trying to run our home. She'd spent those last few days perched by my bedside worrying for me and for our daughters.

This had been her battle too. In that moment, I really believe the fear that had built inside her was released as well. She was fully healed, too. She was having another second chance at our life together. She'd fought for this and now she saw me to the other side. No longer my caregiver, she was going back to being my wife and partner.

I have never slept as sound as I did when I passed out after the "Praise Jesus" moment.

The following morning I awoke.

****

It was around 7:30 am. I was alone and there were no lights on in the room. I was beginning to awaken. Out of the slits of my eyes I could see the room was lit up with a bright orange light. Being attracted to the source of this beautiful light, I rolled my head to the right and began to open my eyes completely. Then I began to smile and stare as a tear rolled out of the corner of my eye.

God had greeted me that morning, just Him and I. He was smiling through the window that morning and touched my face to awaken me before anyone else could. Though the storm was raging the night before, there was the most beautiful sunrise of pinks, blues and oranges coming over the horizon, beaming through the window as a proud Dad. I could feel His warmth touching my face as I just lay there smiling...gazing and soaking in the moment.

I couldn't help but wonder if I had been spared for a reason...

~ 179 ~

I was hurting and broken beyond repair. Then He came along and gave me mercy. It feels like I have been born again, given the gift of a 2nd chance at life.

The haze that I had been living in for so long was gone. I could see clearly again. That slow motion feeling was gone. I was alert and could think clearly.

I was in no pain for three days and on no pain medications. I had been in such agony for so long that this feeling that I was experiencing was like no other.

I couldn't believe it was over. It appeared the God of the universe had seen me through the journey. Now that this saga of my life is over, I can start a new one. But, I still couldn't help but think about some of the things that had happened and wonder, why?

Praise be to God!

Saying:

"Amen!
Praise and Glory
and Wisdom and thanks and honor
and power and strength
be to our God for ever and ever.
Amen!"

-Revelation 7:12

21

Genesis of a Donor

I sat in my room enjoying how I felt for the first time in a long time. A little while later Stephanie came in. "How are you feeling?" she asked. Her voice was tender.

I smiled, "I feel incredible." If a whisper can be exuberant, mine was. I felt great. "I feel like I've been born again. It's like a new life."

"You're not sore?"

"No, really, I feel great."

"Well, your creatinine levels have dropped from about 14 before the surgery to 3."

My kidneys had been functioning at about 2-3% before the surgery. In only 12 hours the new kidney was all the way up to about 30%-40%. The best part was, it would only get stronger. For the first time, in a long time, things were going to get better from here on out.

She kissed my forehead and we talked for a while. The day rolled along with family and friends stopping in to see how I was doing. Things were going great and I felt great. [Did I say that already? I'm sure I said it many times that day, too.]

In another part of the hospital, Tony was doing last minute routine blood work and making preparations for the next day's surgery. The man from Florida getting Tony's kidney had flown up to Toledo with his wife. They were having last minute preparations, too. I was excited for them, knowing how life would change.

The amazing power of medicine and faith were on full display in my room. Where less than 36 hours before the procession in and out of my room had been grim and the prayers were lament and intercession, now my room was full of happy chattering. In the midst of it all, Amy walked in just beaming.

"Troy, you look great," she said.

"Thanks. I feel good."

"The color is back in your face. You were gray when I saw you before the transplant." She folded her arms across the folder she was carrying. "You really needed that kidney. We weren't going to be able to keep you around much longer without it."

Wow. That was something, coming from a woman who worked with this every day. I felt great, but the question about who my donor was gnawed at me. Who was this one-in-four-hundred person?

"Ok Amy, I gotta ask. Who is he? Who is my donor?"

Her smile broadened, "Well, his name is Jay Julian. He's from Colorado Springs, Colorado and he is around 40 years old. He's around 180 pounds."

"Wow, that sounds like me," I said. What were the odds we'd have so much in common? "So is he a big strong rugged fella? A mountain climber or something?" I laughed.

"Well, I can tell you that when I talked to the hospital in Colorado, I told them Jay would be giving his kidney to Jesus."

"Yeah?" I said as we all laughed.

"Jay is a minister from Colorado that was watching a program one night in January and felt a call..."

The Genesis of a donor

In January 2010, Julie (my wife) and I watched the Will Smith's movie "Seven Pounds".

It's a very powerful movie, very moving in a lot of interesting ways. The character Will Smith plays can't forgive himself for something that's happened in the past. The only way he finds forgiveness is by giving of himself, literally, one organ at a time all the way through the movie.

It wasn't so much his story or that there was any connection from my life to that, but it was an awakening.

I didn't know you could be a living donor. It wasn't on my radar. I had never thought about it before, but something woke up inside of me. For the next several nights, I poured myself into researching donation.

I ran across several websites and read some testimonies of people who had been donors and how much they enjoyed it. I also read about how they had progressed physically afterwards. They were still fine and healthy.

I was surprised to learn living donors actually don't have that many ill effects. In fact, what I found was the occurrences of bad side effects are very minute. I think it's about 1 out of 3,000 people who have a major complication.

Kidney donors did especially well.

Then I read a stat that really grabbed me: 18 people a day die on the organ transplant list waiting for a transplant.

I read all this research that says I can donate with very little long-term impact to me. Then, I see people are dying waiting for donors. About that time, I really felt God in my heart saying, "Is this something that you're reading, Jay, or is this something that you're willing to step up and do?"

It wasn't an audible voice; it was just a moving in the Spirit.

Are you willing to count the cost and do it?

I talked to Julie immediately about it. She likes to joke she knew when we "talked" I would dive into it because that's just my personality. Maybe it is. I was already feeling a pull to do it.

She listened, but she was very worried. Kidney donation sounds like major surgery when you tell someone about it. It was hard for her to believe there would not be major risks.

The idea stirred my mind more and more. I was pulled by this passion now. I wanted to do this, so I printed out quite a bit of information from the University of Colorado hospital's website on their living donor transplant program.

I found out their program actually allows people who don't have anybody in mind to donate. So, I called them. I wasn't really sure what to say when I called because it sounded weird even to my ears.

"This may sound crazy," I started, "but can you get me to somebody who would be willing to let me donate an organ, even if I don't know anybody who needs it?"

They said altruistic donation is very rare, but they did it. I had to go through a great deal of testing: physical testing, psychological testing, and lots of milk jugs full of pee that I had to take to Denver.

Finally, about five months after watching the movie, I got the email back from the transplant team saying the doctor said I was a suitable donor. I was also O+, so I was a universal donor.

Then, the real waiting began.

There was nothing I could do at that point but wait. Every test had been done that could be done to that point. It was just a matter of them calling me when they found someone who needed my organ. The need seemed to be so great I thought they'd contact me right away, but as the days passed and no one called, I started to wonder. Then, I started to call.

I started calling every couple of weeks to see if they needed me. They said the right person hasn't called yet.

Then the coordinator sent me an email on Friday before I started a new job. The email said: *I need you to call me because something's come up and it's something we would need to talk about right away.*

I had no idea what was going on. I tried calling and emailing her, but I kept getting voicemail.

The coordinator finally reached me on Sunday, the day before I started my new job. A job I really needed. A job that required my full commitment during training.

Why Do it?

People cannot understand why I'd give a kidney to someone I didn't know. Most were very supportive, they were just curious.

It basically boiled down to a question for me—why not? I really think I've been blessed by God. I've always been called to minister and to serve, and there's no greater love than to serve another person sacrificially.

It's like the Scripture says, "There's no greater love than to lay down your life for a friend."

But see, I'm not even doing that. I'm just giving life to somebody because I can. I didn't want to miss that opportunity. I was glad to do it. I still am glad I did it. I had something I could give. For me it was a small sacrifice—a few weeks of pain and the surrendering of my girlish figure.

For Troy and all of the other people in the chain that has continued on, there is real life in this organ. Lives are being changed. Our small gestures can have a huge impact. And when I offered my obedience, God moved the obstacles for me.

***

"Jay is a Minister from Colorado who was watching a program one night in January and felt led to give his kidney to a stranger."

"Wow." It was incredible. Those of us in the room looked at each other amazed. We were smiling. This miracle was just getting better and better.

We talked about the connections in this life chain. A guy that played Jesus Christ for nine years [me] needed a lifesaving kidney transplant.

The only donor of **12** that could be used was my brother who happens to be a minister. It took a stranger from across the nation to be one of only two matches out of 300. He was chosen and it turned out he was a minister also.

God supplied two donors and they were both Men of God!

What are the odds?!

"No eye has seen, no ear has heard,
no mind has conceived
what God has prepared for those who love him"

-1Corinthians 2:9

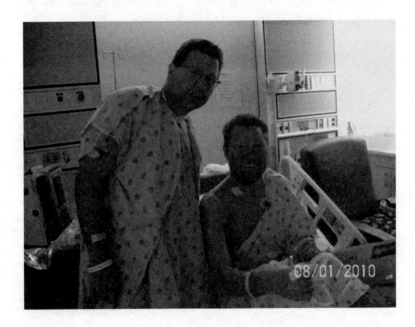

Tony and me

22

The Revelation

It was now the morning of Friday, July 30, and all of the obstacles were gone. I had been given my 2nd chance at life and Tony was about to give his kidney to a man from Florida and change his whole world. Then, this man's wife would drive up to Ypsilanti, MI to give Another 2nd chance to someone there and the chain would continue.

Now it was Tony's turn. For me, waking up meant I had added something. For him, it was having an organ removed. His sacrifice still filled me with awe and gratefulness. Stephanie helped me get dressed and put me in a wheelchair to see Tony off to surgery. The nurses helped wind up all of the tubes and wires and then wheeled me down to where he was waiting.

After being the person needing the help and support for so long, I needed to be there for him, just as he had been for me. I wanted to give something instead of drawing from people.

They wheeled me in the room and Tony was connected to his own set of wires. Marcia was standing next to him while Doc and Susan (Doc's wife) took pictures. Everyone was smiling and chatting. The worst of it was all over. This was now a routine surgery [as odd as it seems] and Tony was a healthy patient.

Down the hall the recipient waited as I had a few days ago. I was thankful to my brother and excited by the recipient's upcoming good fortune.

"Do you want a picture with Tony?" someone asked.

"Sure!"

So with a little help, I got up out of my wheelchair and stood next to him while Susan and others took our picture.

People snapped pictures, said goodbyes, and he went down the hall I'd traveled a couple days before to the operating room.

We sat in the room for a few minutes making idle chit-chat.

"Ready to go back up to your room?" the nurse asked me.

"I'll go with you for a little bit," Steph said and she followed me up. We talked about nothing in particular and watched the clock. The surgery had lasted only a few blinks for me because I was asleep. During Tony's I'd need to wait hours until he came out.

Once he was gone, they took me back to my room and Steph stayed with me for just a little bit. We chatted and watched the clock, then chatted some more.

"Marcia doesn't have anyone down there with her. Are you going to be okay?"

I told her I would be and she promised to come update me in a bit.

A few hours later, Stephanie came back. "It's taking a pretty long time," she said, "I'm not sure what the deal is."

Steph came back with another report. "They came out about an hour ago and said that they had just gotten started."

It didn't make sense, but we had nothing more than theories and speculations and those did nothing for us. It's easy in a moment we cannot control to try to find a way to explain away the confusing parts or to toss around theories. I'm sure Marcia and Stephanie were doing that quite a bit downstairs to pass the time. I was doing it with myself, and most of the theories were not good.

"I'm going back down and wait with Marcia. If I hear anything I will let you know."

She disappeared back out of my room and downstairs to the waiting area with Marcia. They were now three hours in the surgery. I had expected to see him in recovery by now.

Then it was four hours. Then it was five hours. Six hours. I watched the hours slide past with only a couple of calls from Stephanie. I'd learned to trust God and understand timing. Patience is a tough lesson to learn. I'd also had experiences with enough hospitals to know delay was a very bad sign. The theories that had started as unpleasant thoughts had only grown more dire in my own mind as I watched hours continue to tick past. We passed six and went on to seven hours.

At the eight hour mark I was in a panic. No one was coming to give me updates anymore. In fact, the last update from Steph had been at least a couple of hours before. There were no updates from doctors or nurses. I tried to reason he was in post-op and everyone was with him and forgot to tell me, but that wouldn't take hours.

And that didn't match up with what I'd been told in the few updates I had received. She didn't really have anything to tell me, other than they were still waiting. My patience was spent. I was moving to panic.

I started yelling for nurses. "Get me an answer now!"

I knew something's not right. The only hope I could seem to hold on to was the idea that, if he were dead, they would be out talking to us. If they were still in the operating room, he had to be alive.

About ten minutes later, Stephanie walked in to my room. Her face is red and wet from crying. Tears still flooded her eyes and then broke out in rivers down her cheeks. Something was drastically wrong.

My heart dropped down in my stomach. I immediately started thinking the worst. You have got to be kidding me? Is my brother dead? Was he the 1 in 3000 that Doc had spoken of? Could this be possible, that God would spare my life only to take his?

"What's wrong?" I asked with all the strength I could gather for the answer.

"He's okay," her voice cracked. She took a breath and wiped away some tears before she started.

"As soon as they went in, before they even touched the kidney or the cyst, an aneurysm hiding behind the huge cyst burst and they couldn't find it."

She took a deep breath through her mouth and let it back out. I let what she was saying start to sink in. "Doc said he crashed on the table twice and they had to get him back."

Tony had died?

"Honey," Stephanie said through a constant stream of tears. "He's all swollen up and everything right now. They had to give him a bunch of IVs and stuff. He's okay."

Her words didn't really comfort me. In my head I'm thinking, *He's not okay. I almost killed him; it's my fault.*

Then thoughts and questions pounded inside my head.

Maybe he's not going to make it through the night.

What if the aneurysm isn't fixed?

How did they plug it? Would it hold? Did they still do the surgery?

You know how the ideas run through your mind? Fear grabs a hold of you and won't let go. He could still die in the middle of the night. It's not over yet.

No one had mentioned anything Tony had said. Was he unconscious? She said I wouldn't want to see him right now.

She tried to comfort me, "Honey, just think about it. If this wouldn't have happened..."

"No," I said. I wasn't going to hear it. I couldn't think about the happy ending in that moment.

The euphoria of yesterday was shattered by the guilt of that moment. Stephanie just sat down and let me soak it in. I didn't want anyone to talk to me. I was okay, but my brother had nearly died by trying to help me live. That wasn't the sacrifice he'd said he was willing to make.

I started crying. I was crying out of emotions. I was crying to God for answers.

Why did this happen and what was going on?

During the course of this entire trial, I'd asked God where he was going with these setbacks and struggles.

From time to time, He would peel back the curtain and let me see pieces of the plan. He would let me see sparkles of hope. He'd show me a reason for living. He'd create those miracles that let the process jump ahead. All of it had brought us to this? To my brother dying?

Even with the glimmers of hope, each of us gets to a point where you wonder when it's all going to end. God steps in and dusts you off a bit.

I thought about Tony's surgery. I wasn't willing to listen to a thing Stephanie said. I was angry and frustrated and full of guilt. At that moment, there was no comfort. I wasn't thinking through any of it logically. All my mind and emotions said I almost killed my brother. The guilt was intense for about an hour.

Then Marcia came up to my room.

She walked in and I was instantly overwhelmed with a crescendo of intense sadness and guilt when I looked at her. I nearly stole her husband.

She looked at me and my chest clutched. Her face was streaked with the past tears. She pushed back a sniffle with a worn tissue. She walked into the room slowly. I tried to read her emotions but my mind was clouded by my own.

Slowly, she came to me. She leaned forward and wrapped her arms around me without saying a word. She hugged me. Her tears soaked my cheek and ran down to my chin. Her breath was warm on my ear and neck. She spoke in a voice barely above a whisper, "Tony sent me up here to tell you thank you for saving his life."

Then, she stood up and stepped back for a moment. God again lifted the corner of the veil and I saw the sincerity and thankfulness in her eyes that I had not recognized when she came in. Steph continued to stand to the side silently. The two of them exchanged a knowing glance before Marcia turned and left.

I watched her walk out, then turned my head and stared off into the distance. Her words resonated in my mind for a few minutes. "Tony said thank you for saving his life..." I had not seen it that way. I had missed it. I was so caught up in the guilt of the moment and the fear of my brother dying, that I missed the obvious.

It turned out Doc had said to Stephanie "If Tony would not have been the chosen one, he would not have made it through the year," but I didn't let her tell me because I didn't want to hear it.

Then suddenly like slow rain drops at the start of a midday summer shower, blessings of understanding began to come over me.

Numerous times I had asked God "Where are you going with this?" and there would be no answer. Only the test of faith that He was in control and the hope that it was all going to work out.

But for the next hour God rained down on me these blessings of understanding. He gave me the answers to all of the questions I had during the process. He was connecting all of the dots. It felt like a movie playing in my mind of all the things that had led to this event. They were timed perfectly. It now all made sense to me. Even all the way back to when I found out I had the disease, He was preparing the way.

- ☐ He told me about the disease through a life insurance exam that I got because of the birth of my daughter. This was the daughter who would lead me to a church passion drama where I would come to know Christ personally. One year later, I started playing Jesus in that same drama.

- He let me focus on the moment of my salvation every year as I played Jesus in that Passion play.

- He gave me a "Prayer Army" to support me through it all. When the Elders prayed for me in January, Jay Julian was moved by God to give his kidney to a stranger. He had no idea how special and rare his kidney was, but God did. When they prayed in March, the fistula was healed in half the time and my brother, Tony, called out of the blue that week and insisted on giving me his kidney.

- He let our paperwork be delayed by a month so we could be on the fast track to the kidney.

- He showed me Toby was not the plan He had in mind. Though he was a near perfect match; he had had a kidney stone **7 years** prior. That forced me to keep looking.

- He put Toby's wife Debbie in a dialysis center as a nurse a number of years earlier. That opened the door for my treatment and a chance for God to show He heard me. Two hours, two times a week.

- He gave me roughly **12** donors between family and friends to show His love and give me Hope when I needed it.

- He chose Eric to push the process along. Maybe he was Isaac. That would make Tony the ram in the bush...

☐ He gave me a surgeon who was a pioneer in "Paired Donation" to find a kidney.

☐ He gave Tony a full medical workup at no cost to him because the hospital kept finding things to check. [He doesn't have insurance.]

☐ He gave me a wife and two daughters who gave me a reason to fight this battle. He showed us when to push harder, and He showed us when to trust.

☐ He allowed me to be the rare situation in every single case. He stacked the time and odds so far against me that it looked hopeless. Only to cause my Hope to grow stronger in the only thing I had left. Faith! Faith in the sovereign God of the universe to deliver me!

☐ He saved my brother's life by hiding and exposing the aneurism just as it burst.

☐ He allowed me to endure beyond anything I could have ever imagined. Then, just as I reached my limit, He gave me life again.

Those were just the high points. There was so much more.

While I was on my journey up this mountain, on this winding, broken path paved with suffering, God was dropping these seeds along the way. Though at the time, I couldn't see the seeds. I could only see the suffering that was beneath me. My hope was focused on getting to the top of the mountain.

Just as it looked hopeless and I had nothing left, God delivered me to the peak. As I stood there with my arms raised in victory, I turned around and looked down the mountain. When I saw the path I had journeyed, I noticed that same barren broken path I had been traveling for years was now lined with bright, beautiful colors. There were mature trees flowering along with shrubs! There were many flowers of every color and kind lining the cracks of the path. I stood amazed...

It was then I realized those seeds God had been dropping had blossomed into a beautiful reflection of my past. There was beauty in the broken path, joy in the suffering, and meaning in the journey.

I saw two other paths running parallel to mine. It was my brother Tony and my "Blood Brother" Jay; they were on their own paths alongside mine. I could also see how sometimes those roads intersected.

In January, when Jay saw the movie "Seven Pounds", he decided somebody needed his kidney. January 28th was when I stood on the threshold of realization that I'd need a new kidney. I came to my place of surrender and God secured the provision.

We each continued down our own paths of false starts and rejections. We were on the same page in January— although we didn't know each other and we were more than a thousand miles apart.

Then he had another transition period. He was getting tired of waiting and he walked into the clinic and asked if they were going to use his kidney or not. They didn't know he was only two weeks away from "The Call" and I was four weeks from starting my new life.

"Write, therefore, what you have seen, what is now and what will take place later."
-Revelations 1:19

He revealed that this journey was not for me, Jay, or even Tony. It was for you! He had allowed me to experience this miraculous journey to bring glory to Him and Hope to you and others. By sharing this story, you will KNOW! There is a sovereign God in heaven that is performing miracles today, just as He did 2000 years ago when he walked on this earth in sandals.

Have Hope and know the trial you are battling through today may just be the light for someone else tomorrow! The anguish your feeling today will make the Joy that's coming that much sweeter!

But isn't that the way all great things in life are? Without stepping out of the boat and trusting God, you won't have the opportunity to experience the miracle. Gideon wouldn't have defeated the Midianites, Moses wouldn't have led the Israelites out of Egypt, and David wouldn't have defeated Goliath!

"As the Philistine moved closer to attack him, David ran quickly toward the battle line to meet him. Reaching into his bag and taking out a stone, he slung it and struck the Philistine on the forehead. The stone sank into his forehead, and he fell facedown on the ground."   *-1 Samuel 17:48-49*

~ 202 ~

David knew God was for him! Knowing that he RAN at Goliath! That is exactly what we should do. Trust God and take our "Giant" head on.

Know that you have faced challenges before and God was preparing you for this one!

Pray! Pray! Pray that God will guide you and have mercy on you. Then Pray some more!! Surround yourself with encouraging people.

Always be Hopeful in the outcome! Be persistent, relentless, and persevere! Then pray some more.

Know that God is in Control!

And praise God!! Even through the Storm...

Everyone thinks this story is about a surgery and the end. The true story was about the journey getting there. There are people who are right now waiting for their organ. There are others who are waiting to donate. This story doesn't end with one story. It continues on.

This story didn't begin with my surgery or end with it. It began with Jay reaching the end of himself and wanting to help someone else because he felt a call. It continued on through me learning how to surrender this up to God. Then it goes through Tony's life being spared...

And the story keeps on going as the next organ is donated to give "another second chance" to someone down the chain. It continues on to each person who steps up when times get hard and it involves every person who is struggling with that defining moment.

Everyone has a single moment in time when they have to see if they're going to stand up to Goliath or give up. We all have that opportunity to see if we're going to push through.

See, most of us think we're going to be the one to sacrifice. You can see in this story that the truth is, if Tony hadn't stepped up to help me, he would have likely died. In our sacrifices lies our own deliverance. In our giving, we get our return. In our willingness to serve, we are served.

Stranger than Fiction

See, if Hollywood would have tried to write this script, it would have been tossed aside as unbelievable.

But all of these things happened.

By God using Jay to give me a 2nd chance, it allowed others "Another 2nd Chance". Jay and Tony had that opportunity.

And all of you do, too.

What will you do with yours?

Afterwards

We are often asked how I came to know my donor. As a recipient we are only allowed to know as much as our donor wants us to know. Therefore, it was up to Jay to decide when or if he ever wanted to talk to me. I wanted to give him a chance to share how we met since he is the reason we did ever meet. So, once again, I have Jay sharing in his own words.

Jay's Phone Call

A couple weeks after the operation, maybe not even that long, I got a card forwarded to me from the hospital.

It was from Troy and Steph. I let it sit on the table for about a week, maybe two, until Julie asked me one day, "When are you going to call him?"

"I don't know what to say. It's just awkward for me." I didn't donate the kidney to be anybody's hero. I was a bit shy about it. I did want to know how the recipient was doing, but I wasn't sure how to approach the call or what to say, to do. What would be the level of our connection?

I guess you could just say I had to pray up enough till I thought it was the right time. Then, one evening I said to Julie, "I need some quiet. You're going to maybe have to take the boys to do something. I'm going to go give Troy and Stephanie a call."

I still wasn't entirely sure what I could say. I had rehearsed a line to open the conversation, but beyond that I wasn't sure how this would go.

I dialed the number and Troy actually answered. I introduced myself, "Hi, my name's Jay Julian and I'm looking for my kidney."

Troy laughed. He got a kick out of it. Knowing Troy now, I know that was a great opening to our conversation. After that, we had a good long talk for the next hour or so, kind of sharing our stories with each other.

Then, our wives got involved so there were some more tears than normal. It was really cool.

What is also exciting for me is how God just works great things out of it. I would have never expected this story to continue. For me, I thought I would give my kidney to someone who needed it and that would be the end of the story. I was glad to help and I never expected anyone to really know about it. God could use me for one and done. I was so elated about how this happened and so many people got so much out of it.

What if...

There was many times where I faced the prospect of being turned down as a donor. My biggest worry was getting almost all the way and then being turned down. That would have been incredibly disappointing because I WANTED to be used.

But look at what happened afterwards. Donations in the chain have continued and I would have never guessed it would go as far as it has. Those weren't a guarantee, of course, but I was very happy that they might be a possibility.

Then Troy's brother donating really ended up saving his own life. Wow. What a miracle! And then I think when Troy asked—at last count—they have been able to do seven surgeries in the chain from the kidney I donated.

My good friend Pastor Scott Park used the phrase over and over, "It was God's math." You know? And it really was.

When I decided I wanted to donate my kidney, I never would have anticipated any of this happening, but God made all that happen. God orchestrates all that. God makes all the pieces fall into place. What He's really looking for is your participation,

One of the things I want my boys to have as part of their legacy in this family is how we live as Julians. We live with integrity and we live defined by our actions and not our intentions.

****

3 Weeks later

As I [Troy] was recovering at home one day, we received a call from Marcia. She had been notified by NBC News out of Mid-Michigan that they wanted to do an interview with us on this story.

At first I was hesitant, since it was a three hour trip for us to get there and I was still pretty sore. After I thought about the opportunity a bit, and then thought about all that had happened and how it could inspire people, I realized I wasn't so sore that I should miss this opportunity.

It was great to see Tony and Marcia again. Tony was still very sore from the surgery as well. We spent time together at his house while we waited for the news crew.

I love to tell people about all that happened. It gushes out of me. Tony knew this, and he had coached me on what to say and warned me not to go into great detail because the interview would only be a minute and a half.

So, when Jessica Harthorn of NBC 25 Mid-Michigan started the interview with me, she asked "How did you come to need a kidney?" I just smiled and looked around the room at Stephanie, Marcia, and Tony. They all had that look of "Oh no, what's he going to say now."

I started talking and Jessica listened with interest. Not long after I started to share my story, she put down her microphone and just listened to me. The camera never stopped rolling.

Fifteen minutes later, I glanced over at Tony and he was just shaking his head smiling; I had finally finished answering the question.

She looked at me and said, "Thank you for telling me that." She paused for a moment and then continued to ask questions.

They did such a great job on the interview. Later that evening it was the lead story at 6 and 11 on a Sunday night. It turned out really great and the video is linked on my website, if you'd like to see it.

www.anothersecondchance.org

Epilogue

It was now January 2011; I had hoped by now I would be somewhere sharing this story in front of a large group. But nothing had happened. I had told everyone I encountered about this story—whether they wanted to hear it or not. Many people told me to write a book; (shamefully) I had not.

So on my way to work I began to pray to God for an opportunity to share this story publicly in a group setting. I also prayed God would make it crystal clear what exactly he wanted me to do with His story. I was just a construction worker, not an author, but if that is what he wanted me to do, he needed to make it so clear that I could not miss it.

The very next day I received a phone call from a Pastor out in Colorado (Scott Park). He wanted to fly my wife and me out to Colorado Springs as a part of his Sunday message.

He said, "Jay will be up on stage and I will be interviewing him, at some point I will ask Jay, 'How is this guy from Ohio doing anyhow?' Jay will say, 'Well, why don't you ask him yourself, he's sitting right there.' Then you will get up and walk up on stage."

I couldn't believe it! Stephanie and I had been trying to save enough money to fly out to Colorado in the summer to meet Jay and his family, but it hadn't happened yet. I couldn't believe God answered so quickly and with more than I even asked for.

A couple of weeks later on Friday, January 28th, we landed in Colorado Springs. It was six months to the day since I'd had my transplant. We met Jay and Julie on Saturday for lunch. It felt like we were with old friends, telling stories and joking around about all of the things we'd been through.

Sunday was the six month anniversary of Tony's lifesaving surgery. It was also the first time I was up in front of a crowd, sharing our story. Here I was sharing it with Impact Christian Church in Woodland Park, CO.

It was a very special time as Pastor Scot Park did an outstanding message on "Courageous Generosity" during two services. He did a Q&A with Jay, then with me and then with both of us. It was a moment I will not soon forget...

After the first service, I was approached by a number of people asking if there was a book. I always chuckled and told them there wasn't. The entire time I was thinking, "Ok, God, I'm getting the hint". Then a bubbly young lady approached me and asked "Has anyone ever approached you about writing a book?" I chuckled and said, "Yes, but I am no writer."

Then she said, "NO! I am asking you, has anyone ever approached you about writing a book FOR you?"

I sat there with a dumbfounded grin on my face. "No. No one has ever done that... Why? Are you interested in doing that?"

"Yes," she said.

It was at that moment I knew I had no more excuses. When I got home from Colorado, I had a new fire, a new desire to tell this story on a grander scale! I have had the privilege of telling it at a number of churches and events. I started writing the book you are holding in your hands. Though it has not been an easy process by any means, it has been a meaningful one.

But isn't that the way with all great things in life?

"I consider that our present sufferings are not worth comparing with the glory that will be revealed in us"
-Romans 8:18

Acknowledgments

I would like to start by thanking Dr. Rees and the staff at TUMC, as well as the Alliance for Paired Donation. Without this amazing organization I would not be here today. Thank you!

I would like to especially thank all of the courageous Donors that sacrificed their time to get tested for me! Though I don't know who you all are, God does. You gave me light in an otherwise dark time. Thank you.

To my prayer warriors, Army really... Located throughout many Churches in the Fremont area, and as far as Indiana to Georgia, God heard you and answered!!! Praise God! Your prayers mean more to our family than I can articulate here!

A Huge thank you to all of our friends who were there for us during our times of need, and there were many. They say "you know who your friends are when you're down". I found that we had more friends than we knew!

To my co-writer Tiffany Colter, thanks so much for your countless hours of shaping, editing, and writing! Your patience and grace through challenging moments haven't gone unnoticed.

To Eric Suter, my Abraham or is he Isaac? For testing, being chosen, and following through, I say Thank YOU!! You da man!

To my new blood brother Jay, what can I say...Thanks for letting God use you in a MIGHTY way!!!!

They say that "friends come and go, but Family will always be there for you"... These words were never so true! Ted, Tony, Toby, Tracy, and all of your family's, Thanks for testing and being there and caring for me and my family in our moment of need. I love you guys!!!

Dad, Thanks for your years of love and support! Stephanie and I will always cherish you helping out while I healed! And thanks for your faith in allowing this book to become a reality!!! I love you.

Tony, I am not sure whether to say I'm sorry, thanks, or you're welcome... Who knew? All I know is that I thank God every day for what you did and what He did! I love you man.

Stephanie, I love you more now than ever! Thank you for being my caretaker, companion, and best friend. While everything going on around us was scary, you made it a calmer place.

Corrine & Allison, I love you girls more than you will ever know. You're the apple of your ole dad's eye. I am so proud of the both of you and always will be, no matter what! I will always remember the first time I ever held each of you... and watching you grow up to be the beautiful young ladies you are today.

I want you to take this book and cherish it always. Hand it down through our family, for generations to come. Let it be proof that there is a God in heaven and He is still creating miracles today, tomorrow, and forever!!!

Alliance for Paired Donation

The Alliance for Paired Donation was started in August 2006 to help arrange kidney paired exchange transplants. In case you're not familiar with the concept, the basic premise is that someone who needs a kidney has a loved one who is willing to donate one of their kidneys to them, but they aren't a match. So we enroll that pair in a computer database with other people in the same situation. A very sophisticated computer program finds exchanges where the donor for pair one can give to the recipient of pair two, and the second pair's donor gives back to the first recipient. Essentially, they "swap" kidneys. This is a simple two-way exchange, and we always did them simultaneously, to prevent the likelihood that one donor would back out at the last minute.

In late 2006, two colleagues (Utku Unver and Jonathan Kopke) helped me understand that we could, instead, perform chains of transplants by using an altruistic, or Good Samaritan, donor – someone who didn't know anyone in particular who needed a kidney, but just wanted to help save or improve a life through their donation. (Several hundred altruistic donors had done this over the years, but they would just give to one person on a transplant center's waiting list, and that would be the end of it.)

What Utku and Jon helped me see was that if we used these altruistic donors in combination with our incompatible pairs, we could create chains of "pay-it-forward" transplants, where each incompatible pairs' donor pays-it-forward to another needy patient with a willing, but incompatible donor who can continue the chain. What we also realized was that we could perform transplants sequentially, or non-simultaneously, so that these chains were not restricted by the logistic constraints of having to do everything at the same time. In so

~ 215 ~

doing, much longer chains could be formed. We could, in essence, create a "never-ending" altruistic donor chain of transplants.

The transplant community was skeptical. We were warned donors would back out once their loved one got a kidney. We struggled with how to decide who was trustworthy. Ultimately, we decided to give it a try, so on July 18, 2007, Matt Jones (an altruistic donor from Michigan) gave a kidney to Barb in Phoenix. Barb's husband, Ron, was the one we decided to trust – and he didn't let us down. On July 26th, he donated a kidney to Angi in Toledo, and two months later, Angi's mom donated a kidney to George in Columbus. That first chain went on to see 10 recipients transplanted in just over 7 months, and then we had a young woman on the end of the chain who was perfectly willing and able to donate, but she was the rarest of blood types – AB. Amazingly, she waited almost three years before we found someone with whom she matched, and she donated in January 2011, thus continuing the chain.

Chains of transplants are no longer rare – nowadays almost all paired exchange programs arrange them – and it was one such chain that enabled Troy to receive a transplant, and his brother, Anthony, to pay it forward. As you have learned, chains are now used not only to help incompatible pairs, but also to help compatible pairs get a better kidney—like Troy. My hat's off to Troy for sharing his remarkable story, and I hope it brings increased awareness of the option of living kidney donation. I believe we could see as many as 3,000 people a year helped by kidney paired donation, and our future success revolves around the generous men and women who step forward and voluntarily undergo rigorous medical testing and major surgery to help someone else have a better quality of life. But you don't have to give a kidney to help the cause. We offer our services for free, but that doesn't mean it is free. Perhaps

you'd consider giving a financial gift to help us help others. If so, please visit our website at www.paireddonation.org.
---Mike Rees

If you would like to learn more about paired donation or to support the work of the APD, please visit our website at www.paireddonation.org, or give us a call at 419-866-5505. The Alliance for Paired Donation is a 501(c) 3 charitable organization headquartered in Toledo, Ohio. Michael A. Rees, MD, PhD, founded the APD and serves as its CEO and Medical Director. He is Professor of Urology at the University of Toledo Medical Center.

Paired Donation, Your Story and Finding out more.

There is so much more we could talk about here to help others. There are websites that can point you to donation networks if you're facing a transplant [or if you'd like to be a donor]. There are places where you can talk about your story and what you've experienced. There are even more stories I couldn't share here.

All of this and more can be found at our website:

www.Another2ndChance.com

I hope you'll come here and be a part of the community and tell your friends.

Troy

Faith can move Mountains